The Poems
of
Laurence Minot

1333-1352

Middle English Texts

General Editor

Russell A. Peck
University of Rochester

Associate Editor

Alan Lupack
University of Rochester

Advisory Board

Rita Copeland
University of Minnesota

Thomas G. Hahn
University of Rochester

Lisa Kiser
Ohio State University

Thomas Seiler
Western Michigan University

R. A. Shoaf
University of Florida

Bonnie Wheeler
Southern Methodist University

The Middle English Texts Series is designed for classroom use. Its goal is to make available to teachers and students texts which occupy an important place in the literary and cultural canon but which have not been readily available in student editions. The series does not include those authors such as Chaucer, Langland, the Pearl-poet, or Malory, whose English works are normally in print in good student editions. The focus is, instead, upon Middle English literature adjacent to those authors that teachers need in compiling the syllabuses they wish to teach. The editions maintain the linguistic integrity of the original work but within the parameters of modern reading conventions. The texts are printed in the modern alphabet and follow the practices of modern capitalization and punctuation. Manuscript abbreviations are expanded, and u/v and j/i spellings are regularized according to modern orthography. Hard words, difficult phrases, and unusual idioms are glossed on the page, either in the right margin or at the foot of the page. Textual and explanatory notes appear at the end of the text, along with a glossary. The editions include short introductions on the history of the work, its merits and points of topical interest, and also include briefly annotated bibliographies.

The Poems
of
Laurence Minot

1333-1352

Edited by
Richard H. Osberg

Published for TEAMS
(The Consortium for the Teaching of the Middle Ages)
in Association with the University of Rochester

by

Medieval Institute Publications

WESTERN MICHIGAN UNIVERSITY

Kalamazoo, Michigan – 1996

Library of Congress Cataloging-in-Publication Data

Minot, Laurence, 1300?-1352?
    The poems of Laurence Minot / edited by Richard H. Osberg.
        p.   cm. -- (Middle English texts)
    Text comprises Minot's 11 poems found in the 15th century MS
Cotton Galba E.ix.
    Includes bibliographical references.
    ISBN 1-879288-67-2 (pbk.)
    1. Great Britain--History--Edward III, 1327-1377--Poetry.
2. Battles--Scotland--Borders Region--Poetry. 3. Political poetry,
English (Middle) 4. Battles--France--Poetry. 5. Alliteration.
I. Osberg, Richard H., 1947-   .   II. Title. III. Title: Poems of
Laurence Minot, 1333-1352   IV. Series: Middle English texts
(Kalamazoo, Mich.)
PR2085.M5 1996
821'.1--dc20   96-6482
                                                                          CIP

Printed in the United States of America

Cover design by Elizabeth King

Contents

Acknowledgments

Thanks are due to Santa Clara University, which generously provided a Thomas Terry Research Grant for the initial work on this edition. I wish also to thank the Robbins Library at the University of Rochester for supplying me with a copy of Stedman's *The War Ballads of Laurence Minot*, a book which is exceedingly scarce in North America. I am grateful to the National Endowment of the Humanities for its assistance in finishing the volume. I am deeply indebted to my colleague Professor Phyllis Brown for her many valuable suggestions, to my students, especially Richard Winterstein, Hoang-chi Truong, and David van Etten for their extensive assistance in preparing the glossary, and to many colleagues in the Medieval and Renaissance Studies Program for their encouragement. At the University of Rochester Tom Stone, under the supervision of Eve Salisbury, read the manuscript against a microfilm of Cotton Galba E.ix and collated it against several recent editions, an endeavor that led to a number of corrections and textual notes. Eve Salisbury and Jennifer Church were responsible for the formatting of the volume and making corrections. The completed project was then read carefully by Russell A. Peck and Alan Lupack, who assisted generously with the improving of the volume, and by Thomas Seiler and Juleen Eichinger at Western Michigan University, who likewise caught various errors. My greatest gratitude is reserved for Sally and Jerusha for their understanding and support.

The Poems of Laurence Minot

Introduction

MS Cotton Galba E.ix

The eleven extant poems attributed to Laurence Minot celebrate a sequence of English victories on the Scottish border and on the continent between 1333, the Battle of Halidon Hill, and the surrender of the French town of Guînes in 1352. The poems appear to have been written shortly after the events they commemorate; in 6.36, for instance, Minot boasts to the inhabitants of Tournai that King Edward will "breke yowre walles obout," not aware, apparently, that the siege was abruptly raised by Edward in September 1340. In the fifteenth-century manuscript in which the poems are copied, however, they are arranged as a continuous narrative "romance," connected by rubrics and linking stanzas. Other details, too — the title Duke of Lancaster for Henry of Derby in the poem on the naval victory at Sluys, 24 June 1340, a title not conferred until 1352 — suggest Minot may have revised the entire series shortly after completing the last poem in the sequence.

The eleven poems (1017 lines) survive in a single manuscript, Cotton Galba E.ix, a fifteenth-century miscellany that preserves other unique texts of Middle English poetry, the Arthurian romance *Ywaine and Gawayne* and *The Prophecy of the Six Kings to Follow King John* (*The Prophecies of Merlin*) as well as three penitential pieces found elsewhere in the *Cursor Mundi* and other poems more widely disseminated: *The Sevyn Sages of Rome*, the apocryphal *Gospel of Nicodemus*, and the *Pricke of Conscience*. In this aggregate of romance narrative, political prophecy, and devotional material, with its notes on horses and inventory of linen, Cotton Galba E.ix resembles "household miscellanies" like National Library of Scotland Advocates MS 19.3.1 (perhaps owned by the Sherbrooke family) — single-volume libraries that provided information, devotional materials, and entertainment for the instruction and recreation of the family (Turville-Petre, "Some Medieval English Manuscripts," p. 140). The arrangement of the texts (one scribe was responsible for *Ywaine and Gawayne* and *The Sevyn Sages*, a second and third for the short poems on folios 48b through 52a, a fourth scribe for Minot's poems, the *Gospel of Nicodemus* and the shorter penitential pieces, a fifth for the *Pricke of Conscience*) suggests the "pamphlet" construction of similar manuscripts (Boffey and Thompson, p. 283). The

1

name Richard Chawser, written out three times in a modern hand on the last folio, does not, unfortunately, connect the manuscript to Thomas Chaucer and the circle of early humanists, among them, Humphrey, Duke of Gloucester, with whom he was associated, but may be evidence of a sixteenth-century owner of the manuscript.

Cotton Galba E.ix is a large parchment folio 13 x 8½ inches (the original parchment sheets fused onto newer vellum sheets) arranged in quires of twelve leaves each, the ends of the quires being indicated by catch-words. The manuscript is written in two columns to the page, 47–48 lines per column. The scribe responsible for copying Minot's poems into folios 52–57 (usually identified as the fourth of six hands in the MS) went on to copy at fol. 57b the *Gospel of Nicodemus*, and at fol. 67a through fol. 75a, sections of the *Cursor Mundi*, illustrating the process whereby older forms of instructional and devotional writings were reanimated and anthologized for a new generation of readers (Boffey and Thompson, p. 291). The hands and the manuscript have been variously dated; there seems now to be general agreement on the first quarter (Hall, p. ix) to the first half of the fifteenth century (Hulme, *Gospel of Nicodemus*, p. xxii), nearly a hundred years after the Battle of Halidon Hill.

Although nearly all the major fourteenth-century alliterative poems survive only in fifteenth-century manuscripts (Doyle, p. 89), it might well be thought odd that a scribe should care to copy a set of poems describing battles nearly a century old. Wright ascribed the copy of the poems to the interest awakened in the exploits of Edward III by Henry V's successes in France (*Pol. Poems,* I, xxii). Hall notes that *The Prophecy of the Six Kings*, used by the Northern rebels against Henry IV, favors a date prior to the Battle of Shrewsbury in 1403, in which the conspirators were defeated, and he argues that the manuscript compiler would not have included the *Prophecy* later than 1407, a date which marks Henry's decisive victory. On the other hand, specific meanings attached to political prophecy were short-lived. A case in point is the so-called *Prophecy of John of Bridlington*, which in the reign of Edward III was accompanied by an explanatory commentary. In John Capgrave's chronicle, however, two lines are extracted and applied to the execution of Archbishop Scrope in 1404; the earlier interpretation is abandoned entirely (Wright, *Pol. Poems,* I, liii).

Nor should a date later than 1407 for Cotton Galba E.ix be ruled out. Between 1420 and 1425, the child-king Henry VI's uncles, John, Duke of Bedford, in France and Humphrey, Duke of Gloucester, in England, were actively campaigning to uphold the English claim in France. Bedford and Gloucester used both civic pageantry (the coronation of Henry VI in Paris and, on his return to England, the royal entry into London in 1432) as well as poetry (Calot's poem on the succession, posted in France and England) to maintain support for the war party (Osberg, "The Jesse Tree," p. 264). It is in this milieu that James and Simons argue for Minot's poems as dramatic propaganda:

Introduction

In Henry V's reign, and even after Agincourt, the war party had needed such propaganda as "The Libelle of English Policye" to maintain military momentum. By 1425, despite Bedford's steady successes in France (before the tide turned at Orleans in 1429), and Humphrey's warlike posturings at home, a peace party was well established, led from the start of the reign by Cardinal Beaufort. Although we might not expect one of Gloucester's documents to have ended up in the Cotton collection, this avid collector and bibliophile might possibly have been original owner [sic] or might have commissioned Galba E.ix, including Minot, to strengthen the war party in increasingly difficult times. (p. 8)

Supporting evidence for a connection between Humphrey, Duke of Gloucester, and MS Cotton Galba E.ix might be adduced in the addition to the manuscript after 1436 of the poem, "On the Siege of Calais, 1436" (the first seven lines appear on folio 3a; the full poem at 113b, 110b in the older foliation), which honors English valor in the face of French aggression. On the 19th of July, 1436, the Duke of Burgundy laid siege to the city; he was forced to raise it on July 25th:

> The next morow, or yt was day,
> Erly the duk fled oway,
> And with hym they off Gant.
> And after Bruges and Apres both
> To folow after they wer not loth;
> Thus kept they ther avaunt.
> For they had very knowyng
> Off the duk off Gloceturs cumyng,
> Caleys to rescue.
> Bycaus they bod not ther
> In Flanders he soght hem fer and ner,
> That ever may they yt rew.
>   (Wright, *Pol. Poems,* II, 156)

Ironically, the siege was raised not by Gloucester, who was unable to leave England for Calais until July 28, but by his arch-rival Edmund Beaufort. Gloucester did command a *chevauchée* or foray through Flanders in the early days of August, but the poem's partisan enthusiasm rather exaggerates the magnitude of the campaign.

Laurence Minot

Of the poet who names himself Laurence Minot in 5.1 and 7.20 nothing is known with any certainty, and internal evidence from the poems offers only generic hints as to his identity. The poems refer to events between 1333 and 1352, but Minot's presence at all the battles he describes seems doubtful — some poems sound like

3

eyewitness reports, others are "the abstracts and brief chronicles of the time." Minot is quite muddled, for instance, about the French capture of the English cog *Cristopher*, and he places Thomas de Hatfield, Bishop of Durham, at the Battle of Neville's Cross, although the Bishop was in France at the time. Collette concludes from the internal evidence of the poems that Minot was connected with military affairs in the reign of Edward III and that he was especially interested in events on the English-Scottish border (p. viii). Neither Minot's identity nor his purpose as poet can be definitively known, although the early opinions that he was a monk (Ritson) or a priest (Bierbaum) appear unfounded. The view urged by the *Cambridge History of English Literature* and the *Dictionary of National Biography* that Minot was "a professional gleeman, who earned his living by following the camp and entertaining soldiers with the recitation of their own heroic deeds" has been stoutly resisted by his editors, of whom Stedman may be the most partial: it is "extremely likely that he was a Court poet and favorite and not, as has been suggested, merely a vagrant bard following in the track of the English fighting power in France" (p. xi). Recent research on the cultural milieu of Edward III's court has altered somewhat the picture of a court unconcerned with literary and artistic patronage. Juliet Vale sums up this reversal of received opinion:

> Similarly, the absence from this period of surviving illuminated manuscripts associated with the court and the apparent lack of documentary references have led historians to place Edward III, if not in an illiterate, at least in a bookless and artistically unaware milieu. The discovery of a royal library of at least one hundred and fifty volumes underlines the insecure foundations of such assumptions. It is clear, too, that the more important members of Edward's court — Philippa, Isabella and Henry of Lancaster — were also eager to surround themselves with objects of artistic and literary value and it is likely that they differed from other members of the court only in material resources, not in taste. (Vale, p. 56)

Following Vale's lead, James and Simons place Minot in the context of Edward's court, where "a sustained pattern of literary interest" suggests that Minot "should be seen as one amongst the increasingly large retinue of minor functionaries who thronged the later medieval courts and who decided to seek preferment through the production of laudatory poetry in a style which may have appealed to the king himself" (p. 10). Indeed, fresh scholarship has brought to the fore a host of careers in administration and the army enjoyed by lesser gentry from Cheshire and the adjoining counties, particularly with the patronage of Edward's son, the Black Prince, who was Earl of Chester (Bennett, p. 205). Had Minot come to the court or the army under such circumstances, we might well expect an occasional complimentary gesture toward his patron, especially since it was at the Battle of Crécy that the Prince's courage and chivalry first won him universal acclaim. It is a curious feature of

Minot's poems, however, that they fail to mention Prince Edward, a silence singularly odd given the attention they devote to Philip's son, Sir John of France.

By the first quarter of the fifteenth century, at any rate, there is evidence that great magnates like the Duke of Bedford, regent of France, were employing clerk-poets to celebrate their fame, as Lydgate makes clear in his "prologue" to the translation of Laurence Calot's French poem on Henry VI's Title to the Crowns of England and France:

The noble, that worthi varioure,	*warrior [i.e., Bedford]*
Whiche may be callid a very conqueroure,	
Who lyst considre and serche by and by	
His grete emprise in ordre coriously,	*enterprise; zealously*
And specially to encrece his glory,	
Who list remembre the grete high victory	*wishes to*
Which that he had in Vernoille in Perche,	
Fulle notable in boke oute to serche,	
In cronycles to be song and rad;	*sung and read*
And this prince moste discrete and sad,	*serious*
Hy lord of Bedford, of Fraunce the regent,	
Was the first that did his entent,	
By grete advys and ful hy prudence,	*judgment; reason*
Thurugh his laboure and his diligence,	
That made eeoche in cronycle fulle notable,	*everyone*
By the clerk which he knew moste able,	
Renomed of wysdom and science	*Renowned*
Worthie eke of fame and of credence.	*also*
(Wright, *Pol. Poems,* II, 132–33)	

James and Simons speculate about three candidates for Minot's literary patronage, Edward himself, Philippa of Hainault, patron of Minot's contemporary, Froissart, and finally, the old queen Isabella, in retirement at Castle Rising in Norfolk.

One historical document relating to a Laurence Mynotz may in fact lend credence to this last suggestion. Moore prints two documents of 1331 — the only record that has been found of a Laurence Minot roughly contemporary with the poems. These are Latin and French records of the purchase by Laurence Minot in 1320 of a piece (or perhaps more than one piece) of land in Cressy Forest, France, then in the possession of Queen Isabella and recording as well the remission in 1331 by Edward III, to whom the mortgage had passed, of a part of the balance still due.

Although it is by no means certain that the person so named is also the poet, the surname Minot is not a common one in the surviving public records in the late thirteenth and early fourteenth centuries. Hall found traces of six (or perhaps seven)

5

Minots, a number of whom appear to be related to one another; none bears the name Laurence. For the most part, the Minots in the fourteenth century were landed gentry connected with Yorkshire and Norfolk.

Most notable among these is a Sir John Minot associated with various properties in north Yorkshire, including the manor of Thresk. He obtained in 1333 a grant of free warren (a grant from the king for keeping animals) in Carlton, Calton, Hoton, and Skipton-upon-Swale. Sir John owned Carlton Minot (a township, village and parish about thirty-two kilometers northwest of York), the church of which was dedicated to St. Laurence. A person of some local importance, Sir John Minot was named in a return of 1324 as a knight of Yorkshire, and in 1327 he and William Darell were raising forces for Edward's Scottish expedition of that year. In 1338 he is again associated with William Darell, as a witness to a deed by which Darell founded a chantry in Elvedmere church.

Hall thinks that the John Mynyot, Esq., who was a deponent in the Scrope and Grosvenor trial was Sir John's son and heir. The Scrope and Grosvenor trial, at which Chaucer also gave evidence, concerned, as Pearsall says "the determination of a fine point of chivalric privilege," (*Chaucer*, p. 202) and those who gave evidence were among the most celebrated men in England, an indication, perhaps, of the status of the Minot family at this time. In addition to the Yorkshire properties, which John Mynyot extended — he was in litigation, for instance, in 1345 and 1346 over the manor at Islebeck (*Year Books*, R.S. 31, p. 392) — he held land at Bekering in Kent.

Another branch of the Yorkshire Minots is connected with Sir Roger Mynyot, who held land from Eggleston Abbey, near Barnard Castle, in the Wapentake of Gilling West (five kilometers north of Richmond) in 1284–85. Stedman prints notices of a deed by which Richard, son of Richard de Thormodby, gives to Roger Mynyot and Isolda his wife and John his son, and the heirs of Roger, an interest in an Ekelsby property. Roger is probably the person who was lord of a manor at Langale in 1285, held Thurning Manor in 1287, and whose son Jeffry and Catherine, Jeffry's wife, owned a town house in the parish of St. Stephen, Norwich, in 1316. It is worth pointing out that the cult of St. Laurence was well-established early in the north of England — in the seventh century King Oswiu of Northumbria received relics of the saint from Pope Vitalian, in the eighth century the infirmary chapel at Wearmouth was dedicated to him — and it continued to flourish; prior to the Reformation there were two hundred and twenty-eight churches and chapels dedicated to St. Laurence (*The Oxford Dictionary of Saints*, p. 238).

There are records also of Michael Myniot, a prominent London merchant, and Thomas Mynot, "Notaire le Roi," who is probably to be identified with Thomas Minot, Archbishop of Dublin from 1363 to 1375. Interestingly, Thomas Minot was in Flanders on official business at the date of the capture of Guînes (1352).

Introduction

Two pieces of circumstantial evidence serve to link Laurence Minot to the Yorkshire family. First are the stylistic features of alliteration and stanza linking (see Introduction: Minot and the Alliterative Style) associated almost exclusively with Northern and North-west Midlands poems. Second is the dedication by Sir John Minot of a church in Carlton Minot to St. Laurence. While the dialect of the poems seems to be mid-Lincolnshire, some of its features are distinctly Northern, as Hall notes (chief features include the use of *sal* and *suld*, of *ger* and *mun*, the ending of the present indicative plural in *-es*, the present participle in *-and*, the past participle in *-en,* and the use of *at* with the infinitive; the vocabulary, too, has many Northern words). Hall infers that the poet lived on the border between the East-Midlands and the North, suggesting that Minot perhaps belonged to the Norfolk branch of the Minot family, as more recently has Turville-Petre, who infers that Laurence Minot "probably came from Lincolnshire," ("Some Medieval English Manuscripts," p. 129). It is possible then that Laurence Minot was neither an itinerant balladeer nor a court poet (whether minor functionary or favorite of the king) but rather a gentleman-poet of the kind described in the late fifteenth-century *Scotish Feilde* (c. 1515):

> He was a gentilman, by Jesu, that this Jest made,
> which said but as ye see, for soth, and no other.
> At Baguley that burne his biding place had.   *knight; dwelling*
> His auncetors of old time haue yerded their longe   *dwelt*
> before William conquerour this Countrey Inhabited.
>   (Baird, pp. 16–17)

In 1515, Henry Legh was owner of Baguley Hall (near Manchester) and it is likely that he, one of his four younger brothers or his son was the author of *Scotish Feilde* (Baird, p. vii). Other fifteenth-century gentlemen-poets in the Cheshire-Lincolnshire area include Sir Humphrey Brereton of Malpas and Sir Humphrey Newton of Pownall. In Yorkshire, Robert Thornton seems to have been a member of the minor Yorkshire gentry (Thompson, p. 3). Sir Henry Hudson, rector of Spofford, was called on by the York city council to write verses honoring Richard III in 1483 and again in 1486 to have the "making and directing of the shew" for Henry VII's entry into the city (Johnston, *REED: York*, Vol. I, p. 138). All these men are well-versed in the alliterative mode, and Sir Humphrey Newton in particular writes much rhymed alliterative verse in a style the earliest exemplars of which survive from Stanlow Abbey, Cheshire, from the 1270's (Pickering, p. 157). It is clear Newton had read *Sir Gawain and the Green Knight* as well (Robbins, "Gawain Epigone," p. 361). The poetry of these fifteenth-century gentlemen and others, such as John Quixley (another Yorkshire man), Gilbert Banester, and Peter Idley, might suggest that in the fourteenth century "the country squire or town gentleman" (Robbins, "Poems of

Humphrey Newton," p. 123) might also have composed lyrics of similar style and interest (Pearsall, *Old English and Middle English*, p. 226). Perhaps Minot should be thought of, at least in his youth, as a versifying esquire like the knight's son in Chaucer, who "koude songes make and wel endite" (CT 1[A]95).

Minot and Political Poetry

Whether a minstrel in the king's army, a favorite in the king's court, or a versifying member of the Northern minor gentry, Laurence Minot wrote poems whose content and style mark their difference from the popular ballads of his contemporaries, as Collette's comparison of Minot's poem on the Battle of Neville's Cross with Child ballad 159, "The Battle of Durham Field," makes clear. Collette concludes that Minot's poem lacks the distinguishing characteristics of the ballad, "detailed conversation, narration, and action, as well as a sense of immediacy" (p. xxvi). James and Simons argue rather for romance poems as the models for Minot:

> the experience of reading Minot would have been analogous to the experience of reading a short romance, divided into fitts, with appropriate features and generic markers and satisfying the expectations which romances generally fulfilled. The text is thus far from a collection of isolated celebrations but an attempt to unify disparate experiences over a lengthy period through the deployment of an easily recognisable and currently fashionable literary mode. Above all we find an image of patriotic heroism and foreign villainy, an image reflected not in a mirror of chronicle but in a mirror of chivalric romance. (p. 13)

It is inviting to think of Minot's poems as steeped in the conventions and generic expectations of romance poetry, linked to a literary tradition whose continuum extends from the alliterative *Siege of Jerusalem* at one extreme to Chaucer's satiric *Sir Thopas* at the other. Do Minot's poems, however, exhibit the characteristic features of romance? Minot's description of a sea battle provides an interesting test case.

On 30 August 1350, off Winchelsea, King Edward won a significant naval encounter against the Castilian fleet under the command of Charles de la Cerda, a battle known as *Les Espagnols-sur-mer* (poem 10). In the *Alliterative Morte Arthure*, "the Spaniards" who leap overboard at line 3700 have also been thought to allude to the sea-battle off Winchelsea (Finlayson, p. 627; the description of the battle occupies lines 3591–3711 of the *Alliterative Morte Arthure*). A comparison of these two accounts with that of Chaucer's description of a naval engagement between Octavian and Anthony reveals much about general medieval naval tactics and the conventions of the romance *topos* of sea-battles.

3660	Fro the waggand wind out of the west rises,	*When; swaying*
	Brothly bessomes with birr in bernes sailes,	*Suddenly sweeps; force*
	Wether bringes on borde burlich cogges,[1]	
	Whiles the biling and the beme bristes in sonder;	
	So stoutly the fore-stern on the stam hittes	*stern; prow*
3665	That stockes of the steer-borde strikes in peces!	*planks; starboard side*
	By then cogge upon cogge, crayers and other,	*ship; small ships*
	Castes crepers on-cross, als to the craft longes;	*grappling hooks across*
	Then was hed-ropes hewen, that held up the mastes;	
	There was contek full keen and cracking of shippes!	*strife*
3670	Grete cogges of kemp crashes in sonder!	*war*
	Many cabane cleved, cables destroyed,	*cabins*
	Knightes and keen men killed the bernes!	
	Kidd castels were corven, with all their keen wepen,	*Proven; carved*
	Castels full comlich that coloured were fair!	
3675	Up ties edgeling they ochen there-after;	*mast-stays; edgewise; hack*
	With the swing of the sword sways the mastes,	
	Over-falles in the first frekes and other;	*i.e., first blow*
	Many freke in the fore-ship fey is beleved!	
	Then brothly they beker with bustous tackle;	*fight; powerful equipment*
3680	Brushes boldly on borde brenyed knightes,[2]	
	Out of botes on borde, was busked with stones,	
	Bete down of the best, bristes the hatches;	
	Some gomes through-gird with godes of iron,	*pierced; goads*
	Gomes gaylich cledde englaimes wepenes;	*Men; clad make slimy*
3685	Archers of England full egerly shootes,	*Strikes; mortal*
	Hittes through the hard steel full hertly dintes!	*completely cut down*
	Soon ochen in holly the hethen knightes,	
	Hurt through the hard steel, hele they never!	*heal*
	Then they fall to the fight, foines with speres,	*duel*
3690	All the frekkest on front that to the fight longes,	*front rank*
	And ilkon freshly fraistes their strenghes,	*each one*
	War to fight in the fleet with their fell wepenes.	*to fight the battle*
	Thus they delt that day, thir dubbed knightes,	
	Til all the Danes were dede and in the deep throwen!	
3695	Then Bretons brothly with brandes they hewen;	

---

[1] *Weather (wind) brings stout ships against planks (of other ships), / So that the bilge and the beam burst apart*

[2] *Armored knights rush boldly on board, / (Coming) out of small boats on board, (and) were pelted with stones*

Lepes in upon loft lordlich bernes;	*through the air*
When ledes of out-landes lepen in waters,	
All our lordes on loud laughen at ones!	

	By then speres were sprongen, spalded shippes,	*broken; split*
3700	Spanioles speedily sprented over-bordes;	*Spaniards; leaped overboard*
	All the keen men of kemp, knightes and other,	*battle*
	Killed are cold-dede and casten over-bordes;	
	Their swyers swiftly has the swet leved;	*young men; lifeblood*
	Hethen hevand on hatch in thir hawe rises,	*heaving; these gray waves*
3705	Sinkand in the salt se seven hundreth at ones!	

(*Alliterative Morte Arthure*, lines 3660–3705)

Considerably condensed, Chaucer's description nonetheless exhibits similar rhetorical tropes and a comparable grasp of naval tactics:

	And in the se it happede hem to mete.	*chanced them*
635	Up goth the trompe, and for to shoute and shete,	*shoot*
	And peynen hem to sette on with the sunne.	*attack with sun behind them*
	With grysely soun out goth the grete gonne,	*great cannon is fired*
	And heterly they hurtelen al atones,	*fiercely*
	And from the top doun come the grete stones.	
640	In goth the grapenel, so ful of crokes;	*hooks*
	Among the ropes renne the sherynge-hokes.	*hooks to cut rigging*
	In with the polax preseth he and he;	*battle ax*
	Byhynde the mast begynnyth he to fle,	
	And out ageyn, and dryveth hym overbord;	
645	He styngeth hym upon his speres ord;	*point*
	He rent the seyl with hokes lyke a sithe;	*scythe*
	He bryngeth the cuppe and biddeth hem be blythe;	
	He poureth pesen upon the haches slidere;	*peas; slippery deck planks*
	With pottes ful of lyme they gon togidere;	
650	And thus the longe day in fyght they spende	

(*The Legend of Good Women*, lines 634–50)

Chaucer's sea-battle begins with trumpets (compare "Brawndeste brown stele, braggede in trompes," *Alliterative Morte Arthure*, line 3657), and at least two of the maneuvers, grappling the enemy ship and cutting its rigging, are recommended by Vegetius (Allmand, p. 127). By way of contrast, Minot's poem on *Les Espagnols-sur-mer* offers not a single detail of the actual encounter between the English and Castilian fleets, and the generic markers of romance or the *topos* of naval battle are entirely wanting:

10

Introduction

I wald noght spare for to speke, · wist I to spede,　　　*hope to succeed*
of wight men with wapin · and worthly in wede　　　*strong; weapons; armor*
that now er driven to dale · and ded all thaire dede.　　　*grave; dead; deeds*
Thai sail in the see gronde · fissches to fede.　　　*depths of the sea*
5　Fele fissches thai fede · for all thaire grete fare;　　　*Many; vaunting*
it was in the waniand · that thai come thare.　　*waning of the moon (an unhappy hour)*

Thai sailed furth in the Swin · in a somers tyde,　　　*time*
with trompes and taburns · and mekill other pride. . . .　　*trumpets and drums; great*

When thai sailed westward, · tho wight men in were,　　　*those strong; war*
thaire hurdis, thaire ankers · hanged thai on here.　　　*bulwarks; anchors*
15 Wight men of the west · neghed tham nerr　　*approached nearer and nearer*
and gert tham snaper in the snare — · might thai no ferr.　　*made; stumble; get away*
Fer might thai noght flit, · bot thare most thai fine,　　*flee; die (come to an end)*
and that thai bifore reved · than most thai tyne.　　*what; plundered; perish*

Unlike the conventional romance sea-battle, Minot's verse lacks concrete detail (with the exception of "hurdis" [the wooden bulwark on a ship to protect a crew in battle] and "ankers," technical naval vocabulary is absent, and only the alliterative collocation "trompes and taburns" signals the romance battle *topos*), and the engagement itself becomes in Minot's hands merely an occasion to taunt Julius Boccanera, Genoese admiral of the Castilian fleet. In style and tone, Minot's account resembles the account of the Battle of Sluys in the Latin "Invective Against the French":

> *Anglia regna, mundi rosa, flos sine spina,*
> *Mel sine sentina, vicisti bella marina.*
> *Francigenae naves ut aves in rete ruerunt,*
> *Sanguine fluxerunt, lectis caruere suaves.*
> *Anglicus ecce rogus Francos facit hogges et koghes,*
> *Disperiunt, saliunt, dissipiunt, fugiunt.*
> *Chaan seme Chanaan regem pacis fugientem,*
> *Edward Carnarivan dat morti se perimentem.*
> *Dic pos cy pes cy fidei, probitatis, honoris;*
> *Dic pour est ny tremor, error, et arra doloris;*
> *Dic pos cy pes cy, cecidit flos Francigenarum,*
> *Demisit nos cy rex inclitus Angligenarum.*
> 　　(Wright, *Pol. Poems*, I, 35–36)

[Kingdom of England, rose of the world, flower without thorn, honey without sediment, you have won the war at sea.

11

The French ships flew headlong like birds into the snare —
They streamed with blood — choice, pleasant beds.[3]
Behold! The English have made a funeral pyre of the French;
They scatter, they leap about, they disperse, they flee.
Offspring of Chanaan, Chaan was slain by
Edward Carnarvon whom he was attacking.
Tell how few here showed fidelity, probity, or honor.
Tell of dread, bungling, and the promise of mourning.
Tell how here the flower of France fell.
Here the renowned King of England defeated us.]

The Marian typology here associated with England and earlier in the poem with Edward's genealogy (*Est Judaeorum Christus rex sub vice matris,* / *Ergo Francorum rex fiat aper vice matris* [Christ is King of the Jews by succession to his mother. Therefore, let the boar become King of France by succeeding his mother." tr. James and Simons, p. 92]) becomes a standard feature of Lancastrian propaganda, finding its most conspicuous expression in the entry of Henry VI into London in 1432 in the Jesse Tree pageant, which paired the descent of Henry from St. Louis and St. Edward through a woman with the matrilineal descent of Christ. Minot's poems are less obvious than the pageant, but a special relationship between Edward III and the Blessed Virgin Mother is certainly hinted at in lines like "And Mari moder of mercy fre, / save oure king and his menye" (4.10–11) and "Mari, have minde of thi man · thou whote wham I mene. / Lady, think what I mene — " (11.4–6).

It was widely believed, of course, that victory in battle was a direct manifestation of the divine will, and Minot's frequent invocations of God, Mary, and the Holy Ghost are the reverse coin of his fervid patriotism and his vilification of the Scots and French — a testimony to the righteousness of Edward's cause. Not yet had general weariness with the war or the clerical pacifism associated with Wycliff and with Lollards like William Swynderby made themselves felt. Edward laid claim to the crown of France in 1337 and formally assumed the title of King of France in January of 1340. For Minot, the unbroken string of victories at home and abroad was validation of the justice of Edward's claim.

Latin verse, too, offers stylistic parallels, particularly alliteration and stanza-linking, with Minot's, as in this passage from "Poem on the Scottish Wars from the Time of Edward I":

---

[3]This seems to be an ironic reference to death.

12

Introduction

Veniet rex Angliae manu non occulta,
Multa super Priamo rogitans, super Hectore multa.
  Multa sibi cumulat mala gens superba,
Anglicos ad praelia provocans acerba;
  Verbera cum venient, tunc cessabunt verba:
Cum totum fecisse putas, latet anguis in herba.
  ["Non latebite," inquiunt, "nobis luce Phoebus;
Per nos ruent Anglici simul hiis diebus,
Nullus pervilibus percel speciebus." (?)
Ludit in humanis divina potentia rebus.
  O Die potentia! te pro tuis peto!
Anglis in auxilium veni vultu laeto!
Regis causam judicas, gratiam praebeto:
Tu sine principio non vincere falsa jubeto.]
  (Wright, *Pol. Songs*, p. 172)

[The King of England will come with open force,
inquiring much about Priam and much about Hector.—
  The proud people raise a heap of evils for themselves,
provoking the English to the bitter contest;
words will cease, when the blows come;
though you think you have finished entirely, there is a snake concealed in the grass.—
  ["The sun," they say, "will not be concealed from us with his light;
the time is come when the English will all fall by our hands;
no one . . . . . "
The Divine power plays with the prospects of men. —
  O power of God! I petition thee in favour of thy people!
come with a propitious countenance to the aid of the English;
judge the king's cause, and give him grace:
thou who art without beginning, do not let falseness triumph.]]

Collette points out that Minot's poem on the Battle of Neville's Cross is very close to a contemporary Latin poem on the same subject, even to the metaphor of flowers that have fallen:

Si valeas paleas, Valoyes, dimitte timorem;
In campis maneas, pareas, ostende vigorem.
Flos es, flore cares, in campis viribus ares,
Mane techel fares, lepus es, lynx, non leo pares.
Francia flos florum, caput olim nobiliorum,
Jam contra mores leopardus tollit honores.
Subpedito florem, rapio florentis honorem,

13

The Poems of Laurence Minot

Flos fueram, formido feram cum jubare veram.
    (Wright, *Pol. Poems,* I, 40)

[If you are worth anything, Valois, put aside fear. Stay in the field, be obedient, display your energy. You are the flower, you have lost the flower, your strength has dried up; *Mane, Techel, Phares.* You are a horse, a lynx: you do not look like a lion. France is the flower of flowers, the capital once of those of nobler birth. Now, against his nature, the leopard carries off the honours. I supply the flower, I seize the glory of him that prospers. Once I was the flower; now I fear the real beast with its splendour. Tr. James and Simons, p. 96]

In addition to Latin political poems, Minot's poetry does bear comparison with a number of English homiletic and satiric poems, notably those found in MS Harley 2253, "Erthe fro erthe" and "Weping haueth myn wonges wet," as well as poems also called, often loosely, "political" like "The Song of the Husbandman" and "Satire on the Consistory Courts," but which are perhaps better understood as "estates satire" (Kane, p. 82). Turville-Petre notes too that the "Lament for Sir John Berkeley" has close stylistic affinities to Minot's poems ("Some Medieval English Manuscripts," p. 129). The clearest parallels, however, are to battle descriptions in "The Flemish Insurrection" (MS Harley 2253), a poem about events of 1302:

this frenshe come to flaundres so liht so the hare,	*as nimble as*
er hit were mydnyht hit fel hem to care;	
hue were laht by the net so bryd is in snare,[4]	*they; caught*
with rouncin & with stede.	*horse*
the flemmisshe hem dabbeth o the het bare;	*strike; head*
hue nolden take for huem raunsoun ne ware;	*they would not*
hue doddeth of huere heuedes, fare so hit fare,	*cut off their heads*
Ant thare-to haueth hue nede.	
(Robbins, *Hist. Poems,* p. 12)	

Another Harley poem recounting events of 1306, "The Execution of Sir Simon Fraser," also seems to anticipate themes in Minot — the "fals foreward," the pride of the Scots brought low, the severity of battle:

To the kyng edward hii fasten huere fay;	*they; their faith*
fals wes here foreward so forst is in may,	*their promise, frost*
that sonne from the southward wypeth away:	
Moni proud scot ther-of mene may	*lament*
to ȝere.	*this year*

---

[4]This figure is to be found in the Latin poem on the Battle of Sluys as well as in Minot's poem 10.16 — "snaper in the snare."

Nes neuer scot-lond   *Never was*
with dunt of monnes hond   *blow (dint); man's*
allinge aboht so duere.   *wholly paid for so dearly*
    (Robbins, *Hist. Poems*, p. 15)

The poem's final stanza too offers themes to be heard again in Minot's poems — the linkage of Scots perfidy with French encouragement, the poet's derision of England's enemies ("tprot" as an exclamation of contempt), and the power of Edward I (he of the "longe shonkes") to subdue his enemies:

the traytours of scotlond token hem to rede,   *counsel*
the barouns of engelond to brynge to dede;   *death*
Charles of fraunce, so moni mon tolde,   *many men said*
with myht & with streynthe hem helpe wolde,
    his thonkes!   *Thanks to him!*
  Tprot, scot, for thi strif!
hang up thyn hachet ant thi knyf,
whil him lasteth the lyf
with the longe shonkes.
    (Robbins, *Hist. Poems*, p. 21)

Finally, Minot's poems share certain narrative techniques with partisan, political poems in Latin, Anglo-Norman, and Middle English, techniques like sudden jumps in time and abrupt changes of subject (Kendrick, p. 187). The opening of the poem on the Battle of Neville's Cross, for instance, may refer to the Battle at Dupplin Moor, in which Edward Balliol and "the Disinherited" defeated the Scots on 12 August 1332, although the poem leaps abruptly to 17 November 1346 after the fifth line. Kendrick notes that such abrupt changes "are fairly common in medieval political verse because the poet uses the juxtaposition of present and past events to suggest analogies that he then uses to imply criticism of his opponents" (p. 187). Another technique of political poetry, the practice of alluding to earlier political poems (Scattergood, pp. 163–64), occurs in Minot's poems as well; in 6.3 and 7.2 Minot alludes to *The Prophecy of the Six Kings to follow King John*, the prophecy of Merlin, in which Edward III is identified as the boar and the lion.

As late as 1415, poets continued to celebrate English victories in France in a poetry whose style has clear affinities with Minot's. The famous Carol of Agincourt, preserved because a scribe, wearied of transforming alliterative poetry into prose chronicle, finally just copied out the end of the poem, demonstrates many of the hallmarks of Minot's style — alliteration, the denomination of Henry V as "oure lord the kynge," generalized battle description, God's help in victory:

Stedes ther stumbelyd in that stownde,	*moment (vicissitude)*
that stod stere stuffed under stele;	*stout well-padded*
With gronyng grete thei felle to grownde,	
Here sydes federed whan thei gone fele.[5]	
Owre lord the kynge he foght ryght wele,	
Scharpliche on hem his spere he spent,	*them*
Many on seke he made that sele,	*sick person; made well [by killing him]*
Thorow myght of god omnipotent.	

    (Robbins, *Hist. Poems*, pp. 75–76)

Its ironic deprecation of the enemy, its plain language and heavy alliteration attest to the continued vigor of alliterative battle poetry in an age otherwise dominated by aureate rhyme royal.

Minot and the Alliterative Style

As the dates of the battles (1333–52) he commemorates suggest, Laurence Minot must have been nearly a contemporary of Geoffrey Chaucer, but no one today is likely to subscribe to the view of him put forward by his first editor, Joseph Ritson:

> one may venture to assert that, in point of ease, harmony, and variety of versification, as well as general perspicuity of style, Laurence Minot, is, perhaps, equal, if not superior, to any English poet before the sixteenth, or even, with very few exceptions, before the seventeenth century. (p. xiii)

In fact, modern readers are more likely to connect Minot with the unflattering portrait of court poets found in the Prologue to *Wynnere and Wastoure*:

Bot now a childe appon chere, withowtten chyn-wedys,	*face; beard*
That never wroghte thurgh witt thies wordes togedire,	*shaped*
Fro he can jangle als a jaye and japes telle,	*knows how to; jokes*
He schall be levede and lovede and lett of a while	*believed; esteemed for*
Wele more than the man that made it hymselven.[6]	*composed the poem*

    (lines 24–28)

In most contemporary surveys of medieval English literature, Minot's poems enjoy at best passing notice: "Indeed, one reason for Minot's unpopularity with his critics

---

[5]When they began to feel their sides feathered with arrows.

[6]*Wynnere and Wastoure and the Parlement of The Thre Ages*, ed. Warren Ginsberg (Kalamazoo: Medieval Institute Publications, 1992), p. 14.

is his fierce, sardonic nationalism, noticeable in his unwavering prejudice against the Scottish-French alliance." That he "can jangle als a jaye," however, nearly always invites comment: "Abundant alliteration was a snare to any transitional poet with Minot's journalistic cast of mind, which reveals itself in trite phrases and a want of feeling for heroic simile and metaphor" (Partridge, p. 293).

While hyperbolic, Ritson's comments are worth a second glance, for they underline features of Minot's poetry too long neglected — the variety and ingenuity of Minot's prosody. As "a Southren man," Chaucer's Parson claims he "kan nat geeste 'rum, ram, ruf,' by lettre" (CT X[I]43), a line whose unhappy effect has been to polarize, however unconsciously, the treatment of alliterative long line verse (Northern, Francophobic, provincial) and accentual-syllabic verse (courtly, urban, Ricardian). Minot is the only fourteenth-century poet known to us whose poems are comfortably composed in both styles. It should be noted that the metrical principles of Minot's rhymed long lines (see poems 2, 5, 9, 10, and 11, frequently referred to as "alliterative long line") do not conform to the rules of the unrhymed long-line poems of the Alliterative Revival (see Cable and Duggan); their tumbling rhythms do resemble, however, those of the Harley lyrics (see Osberg "Alliterative Technique," pp. 143–45).

Traditional Alliterative Vocabulary

Minot's poems employ the vocabulary of traditional alliterative collocations, many of which they share with the rhyming romances and poems of the Alliterative Revival, as a number of editors following Hall have suggested: "In Minot, who is certainly early fourteenth-century, there are similar stock phrases — 'wight in wede,' 'suth for to say,' 'loud or still,' 'fers and fell,' 'mirth on mold.' The absence of any large body of earlier thirteenth-century ballads, in which the conventions could have been worked out, is puzzling" (Robbins, *Hist. Poems,* p. xxxiv).[7] Examination of Minot's collocations reveals, however, that they owe no special debt to the distinctive vocabulary of alliterative long-line poems or rhyming romances; Minot's alliterative vocabulary has more in common with the language of the York plays and Middle English lyrics than it does with that of *Wynnere and Wastoure* or *The Siege of Jerusalem.*

The eleven poems contain three hundred twenty-four alliterative collocations, a few

---

[7]Collette provides a fairly complete list of Minot's alliterative collocations and lists of other works in which they also occur. Many of the phrases for which she could find no parallels do occur in lyric poems and the York plays — *cares cold, with dole er dight, gaudes and gile, hunt als hund dose hare,* and so on. These phrases are listed in the Notes following the text.

more than half of which (one hundred sixty-seven) are unique to these poems, for instance "biging bare," 7.123; "brenis bright," 6.3; "diner was dight," 11.22; "letherin ledderr," 11.19; "met on the more," 9.4, and so on.

Of the one hundred fifty-seven collocations found in other poems (the recurring phrases), forty-four (28%) survive from Old English poetry and prose or from Early Middle English poetry (see Oakden and Fifield). These are the alliterative commonplaces, "bute [bote] of all my bale," 1.4; "king with croune," 7.170; "suth to say," 3.71; "trey and tene," 6.2; "werldes wele," 8.16, and may be found in the poems of Chaucer and Gower as well. Forty-seven additional collocations (30% of the recurring phrases) are shared with the rhyming romances and poems of the Alliterative Revival, phrases like "bale betes," 2.28; "knightes kene," 4.52; "crakked many a crowne," 1.59; and "mekill might," 7.12. It is misleading to think on the basis of these shared phrases, however, that Minot is writing in the tradition of the rhyming romances or poems of the Alliterative Revival, for only nine of these phrases (5% of the recurring phrases) are to be found elsewhere exclusively in the rhyming romances and poems of the Alliterative Revival. These nine collocations are identified in the Notes.

On the other hand, sixty-four of the collocations (40% of the recurring phrases) occur elsewhere only in the Middle English lyrics and the York plays, collocations like "bargan dere thai boght," 7.64 ["this bargan sall be bought," *York Plays* 9 (Noah and his Wife): line 126]; "care es cumen," 8.8 ["oure cares ar comen," *York Plays* 6 (Adam and Eve driven from Eden): line 46]; "cant and kene," 7.107 ["cant and kene" *York Plays* 22 (Temptation of Jesus): line 184], or "done thaire daunce," 1.66 ["that daunce is done," *York Plays* 19 (Massacre of the Innocents): line 96]. These collocations have likewise been identified in the Notes. It should be observed that half of the collocations shared between Minot's poems and the rhyming romances also occur in the York plays and the lyrics; in all, one hundred thirty-one of the one hundred fifty-seven recurring alliterative phrases (83%) are to be found in the plays and the lyrics. This is not a vocabulary much employed by Chaucer or Gower (some twenty-eight of the collocations also occur in Chaucer and Gower; these are the most traditional and widely occurring of the collocations and coincide, for the most part, with those phrases surviving from Old and Early Middle English poetry); it is the vocabulary of a popular poet writing in a tradition of lyric alliterative composition, a poet whose audience must have been one much like that assembled for the Corpus Christi plays, one not exclusively courtly or learned but composed of all stations and estates.

Introduction

Minot's poems are written in the accentual-syllabic tradition of most Middle English lyric poetry. The line is generally composed of homomorphic alliterative half lines either with predominantly one unstressed syllable between stresses corresponding to the major lexical stress (meter A; poems 1, 3, 4, 6, 7, 8) or with mostly two or three unstressed syllables between stresses (meter B; poems 2, 5, 9, 10, 11, a group which also shares a common stanza form). The contours of the half-lines conform to phrases and small grammatical units; in the following examples, alliteration also distinguishes the half-lines [s=strong stress; w=weak stress; S=stressed alliterative figure]:

Meter A

Oure *k*ing was *c*umen, *t*rewly to *t*ell (3.11) wSwSw SwwS

*p*rinces and *p*ople ald and yong (3.19) SwwSw sws

thai *s*oght the *s*tremis fer and wide (3.73) wSwSw sws

Thai *f*aght ful *f*ast both day and night (3.103) wSwS wsws

*s*uld he *s*chew ful *m*ekill *m*ight (7.12) SwS wSwS

*g*rant him *g*race of the Haly *G*aste (4.8) Sws wwswS

Meter B

he has *c*rakked yowre *c*roune, wele *w*orth the *w*hile (2.11) wwSwwS wSwS

*R*ughfute *r*iveling, now *k*indels thi *c*are (2.19) SwSw wSwwS

and have *N*ormondes i*n*ogh to *l*eve on his *l*are (5.9) wwSwwS wSwwS

with mani *m*ody *m*an that *th*oght for to *th*rive (5.42) wwwSwS wSwwS

was *c*omen into *C*agent *c*antly and *k*ene (5.64) wSwwwSw SwwS

when he was *m*et on the *m*ore · with *m*ekill mischance (9.4) wwwSwwS wSwws

At the West Minster hall · suld his *s*tedes *s*tonde (9.11) wwswws wwSwS

bot with *s*chipherd *s*taves ·*f*and he his *f*ill (9.20) wwSwSw SwwS

thai *r*obbed and thai *r*eved · and *h*eld that thai *h*ent (9.24) wSwwSw wSwwS

Thare was sir *D*avid · so *d*ughty in his *d*ede (9.39) swwSw wSwwwS

Thai *s*ail in the *s*ee gronde ·*f*issches to *f*ede (10.4) wSwwSw SwwS

Ye *b*roght out of *B*retayne · yowre *c*ustom with *c*are (10.25) wSwwSw wSwwS

Both the *l*ely and the *l*ipard · suld *g*eder on a *g*rene (11.3) wwSwwwSw wSwwwS

Thare *g*retes thi *g*estes · and *w*endes with *w*o (11.29) wSwwSw wSwwS

Alliteration is principally decorative, coinciding frequently but not inevitably with the major lexical stresses of the phrase. Although half lines are often linked by alliteration, Minot sometimes subordinates lexical stress and alliteration to the requirements of ictus (stress) elevation.

19

he *gaf g*ude confort on that plaine (1.83) wSwsw sws
Thai fand the *galay* men grete wane (3.93) wswsw sws
and *f*olk for *f*erd war *fast f*leand (7.90) wSwS wSws

Minot also promotes pronouns, prepositions, even occasionally copulas to ictus:

pronouns:
    of **tham** that war so *s*tout on *s*tede (1.54) wsws wSwS
    ogaines **him** with *s*cheld and *s*pere (1.14) wsws wSwS
    On Filip Valas fast cri **thai** (1.69) wswsw sws

prepositions:
    Jhesu **for** Thi woundes five (1.91) sws wsws
    that **in** that land than had no pere (3.14) wsws wsws

copulas:
    and the galaies men also (3.51) swswsws
    both in yren **and** in stele (3.102) swsw sws
    in Fraunce **and** in Flandres both (3.6) wS w?s wSws

Another difficulty in Minot's prosody, raised in line 3.6 above, regards the treatment of inflections, particularly the genitive singular in monosyllabic nouns, *-es*, in plurals, *-is*, *-es*, and, most vexed, final *-e*. It is clear Minot relies on inflected verbs, *-es*, *-ed* and *-en* for medial unstressed syllables in many lines:

Listens now and lev**es** me (3.117) Sws wSws
Thai hov**ed** still opon the flode (3.121) wsws wsws
and rev**ed** pouer men thaire gude (3.122) wswsw sws
thus have ye wonn**en** werld**es** wele (8.16) wswSw SwS

and so too plural inflections:

Now God that es of might**es** maste (4.7) wsws wSwS
with lord**es** and with knight**es** kene (4.52) wsw swSwS

In some instances, "Furth he ferd into France" (4.19), for example, it is clear the scribe has rendered the disyllable "fered" as a monosyllable or in 7.18, "for a nobill prince sake," that the possessive suffix has been elided. Such syncope is not, however, unusual. In 6.15, "The harmes that ye have hent," *harmes* is probably monosyllabic in a trimeter line as is *dintes* in 6.34, "of dintes ye may yow dowte." *Harmes* is disyllabic in 6.43, "Yowre harmes cumes at hand"; moreover, Minot does not rigorously avoid double unstressed syllables in meter A:

than likid him no langer to lig (7.80) wSws wSwwS
over that water er thai went (7.82) SwwSw SwS
for to fell of the Frankisch men (7.86) SwS wwSws

Even when syncope is assumed, "kayes of the toun to him er gifen" (8.88), double unstressed syllables between stresses occur. In short, it is impossible to say precisely under what conditions syncope may be invoked; in meter A, however, generally no more than two unaccented syllables are permitted between stresses.

Likewise, final -*e* in meter A is apparently an unstressed syllable when required:

that it mun be ful dere boght (3.119) wsws wsws
Than the riche floure de lice (4.25) swsw sws
a *ste*de to um*st*ride (4.69) wSwswS
of a grete clerk that Merlin hight (7.2) wwsws wsws
*h*ende God that *h*eried *h*ell (7.34) Sws wSwwS
Franche men *p*ut tham to *p*ine (7.77) sws SwwS

Occasionally, before a following vowel where elision normally occurs, final -*e* cannot be sounded, giving rise to a so-called clashing stress:

with *b*rade ax and with *b*owes *b*ent (7.84) wSs wwSwS

As might be expected, clashing stress in meter A is rare; usually, the scribe has failed to provide etymological final -*e*:

for *d*ern[e] *d*edes that *d*one me *d*ere (1.10) wSwSw wSwS
of wild[e] Scottes and alls of tame (1.60) wsws wsws
the *f*als[e] *f*olk of Normundy (7.72) wSwS wsws
With *b*ent[e] *b*owes thai war ful *b*olde (7.85) wSwS wswS

There is some indication, however, that in first half-lines in meter A Minot allows a type of rising-falling rhythm, x/\x:

for *h*elp Scotland gan thai *h*ye (1.22) wwSsw swS
on the *E*rle *M*orré and *o*ther *m*a (1.42) wwSSw wSwS
that *w*ist both of *w*ele and *w*o (3.52) wSs wSwS
The right aire of that cuntré (4.28) wss wsws

A similar feature of Minot's metrics is the so-called "broken-backed line," in which a caesura separates two strong stresses mid-line:

*f*aght wele on that *f*lude — *f*aire mot him *f*all (5.78) SwwwS SwwS
*W*ight men of the *w*est · *n*eghed tham *n*err (10.15) SwwwS SwwS
all thise *I*nglis men *h*armes he *h*etes (2.26) wwSws SwwS

21

bot galay *m*en war so *m*any (3.105) wswS swSw
that Inglis men *w*ex all *w*ery (3.106) wsws SwSw
Two hundreth and mo *s*chippes on the *s*andes (5.71) wswws SwwS
had oure *I*nglis men won with thaire *h*andes (5.72) wwSws swwS

A hallmark of unrhymed alliterative long line verse, clashing stress in second half-lines seems not to occur with any frequency in Minot's poems. It is instructive that the only indisputable evidence for a clashing stress in the second half-line in Minot's poetry is in meter A:

when *h*e did fell his grete *o*kes (4.62) wSws wsS

There is little evidence in either meter A or meter B that clashing stress in the second half-line is metrical:

with erles and barons and many *k*ene *k*night (5.26) wswsw wwwSS?
bot *f*one *f*rendes he *f*indes that his *b*ale *b*etes (2.28) wwSwwS wwSSw?

In both these lines, however, final -*e* may be sounded, wwwSwS, wwSwS. In fact, Minot's metrics seem more like those of the alliterative poems of MS Harley 2253 than like those of the unrhymed alliterative long line poems, as do his stanza forms.

Stanza Forms

The variety of Minot's metrical effects is mirrored in the heterogeneity of his stanza forms, especially those poems composed in meter A:

1. 92 lines in eight-line stanzas, abababab with stanza linking
3. 126 lines in couplets
4. 96 lines in six-line tail-rhymed stanzas, aa^{4}b^{3}cc^{4}b^3
6. a flyting in six three-stress eight-line stanzas, abababab, followed by three eleven-line stanzas, ababababcac, the first c rhyme being a bob line.
7. 173 lines in eight-line stanzas rhymed ababbcbc with stanza linking. The four introductory stanzas are in a different form, two six-line stanzas rhymed aabbcc alternating with two eight-line stanzas rhymed aabbccbb.
8. 96 lines in eight-line stanzas rhymed ababbcbc with stanza linking, the form used in poem 7.

Despite some variations (due perhaps to revisions), the poems in meter B all exhibit the same stanza form:

2. 30 lines in six-line stanzas, aaaabb with linking between the frons (aaaa) and cauda (bb).

5. 88 lines in various stanza forms; predominant is the six-line stanza found in poem 2, aaaabb with linking between the frons and the cauda, (7 stanzas). There are as well three monorhyming stanzas of six lines, five of four lines, and one stanza of eight lines, aaaaaabb with linking between frons and cauda.

9. 66 lines in various stanza forms. Predominating is the six-line stanza aaaabb with linking between the frons and cauda (5 stanzas). There are two eight-line stanzas aaaaaabb with stanza linking between frons and cauda, two monorhymed four-line stanzas, and two six-line monorhymed stanzas, one of which has linking between the fourth and fifth line.

10. 30 lines in six-line stanzas rhymed aaaabb with linking between the frons and cauda.

11. 40 lines in six-line stanzas rhymed aaaabb with linking between the frons and cauda.

Minot's alliterative phrase "hunt als hund dose hare" (8.21) occurs only in one other extant poem, the "Song of the Husbandman" (c. 1300) from MS Harley 2253:

> thus the grene wax us greveth under gore,
> that me us honteth ase hound doth the hare.
>
> he us hontethe ase hound hare doth on hulle;
> seththe y tek to the lond such tene me wes taht.
> (Robbins, *Hist. Poems*, pp. 8–9)

Such stanza-linking, found in Minot's poems 1, 4, 7, and 8 (concatenation) is a feature of much Northern alliterative verse, particularly six rhyming romances: *Sir Perceval of Galles*, *The Awntyrs of Arthur*, *Sir Degrevant*, *The Avowynge of Arthur*, *Sir Tristrem*, and *Thomas of Erceldoune* (Medary, p. 244). It is also to be found in *Pearl*, "A Ballad of the Scottish Wars," and in a number of poems from MS Harley 2253 in addition to "The Song of the Husbandman": "Middelerd for mon wes mad" (Brook, #2); "Weping haueth myn wonges wet" (Brook, #6); "In a fryht as y con fare fremede," (Brook, #8); "A wayle whyt ase whalles bon" (Brook, #9); "Heȝe Louerd, thou here my bone" (Brook, #13); "Wynter wakeneth al my care" (Brook, #17); as well as occasional stanza-linking in "Ase y me rod this ender day" (Brook, #27), and "God, that all this myhtes may" (Brook, #29). There is as well in MS Harley 2253 a long Latin poem in alliterative monorhyming quatrains with stanza-linking, composed soon after 1298, perhaps at Alnwick ("Poem on the Scottish Wars from the time of Edward I," Wright, *Pol. Songs*, p. 160), and a thirteenth-century Latin poem written near Durham, which exhibits both alliteration and stanza-linking (Hall, pp. 112–20). The Scottish alliterative poems, *The Buke of the Howlat*, *Rauf Coilȝear* and *The Pistel of Swete Susan* share a common stanza form (found also in *The Awntyrs* and *Golagros* and "The Song of the Husbandman") and some stanza linking. The *Susan* stanza is also to be found in *Somer Soneday*, which links both stanzas and the frons and cauda of individual stanzas by iteration. Stanza-linking in the alliterative York plays, at least one of which, 46: "The Appearance of Our Lady to Thomas," shares the stanza-form of the Scottish poems, is fairly consistent as well; in 40: "The Travellers to Emmaus" linking is perfect throughout.

Whatever its origin, whether of French, Latin, Welsh, or of native provenance, concatenation belongs almost exclusively to Northern poetry where it occurs in connection with alliteration. It makes its earliest appearance in English in popular songs of the late thirteenth century, popular songs like "The Song of the Husbandman" which may well have provided Minot models for composition.

In addition to stanza-linking, Minot's poems also exhibit the somewhat less common feature of iteration, verbal repetition linking one rhyming section of the stanza (frons) to a shorter "tail" section (cauda). In *The Awntyrs*, the eighth verse is linked to the ninth by iteration, but otherwise this technique is not to be found in the rhyming romances. In the poems of MS Harley 2253, however, iteration plays a role, not only in a complex stanza like that of the "Satire on the Consistory Courts" (Robbins, #6), whose tail-rhyme frons aa^4b^3 cc^4b^3 dd^4b^3 ee^4b^3 is linked to the cauda $ffgggf^3$ by repetition, but also in stanzas similar to Minot's, as for instance "Ichot a burde in a bour" (Brook, #3), aaaaaaaa bb with linking between lines 8 and 9, and "Weping haueth myn wonges wet" (Brook, #6), rhyming abababab cdcd with linking between lines 8 and 9. Iteration is also found in "Middelerd for mon wes mad" (Brook, #2), rhyming abababab cbc, again with linking between lines 8 and 9. All of Minot's poems in meter B exhibit iteration between the monorhyming frons and the cauda.

Such devices as alliteration, concatenation, and iteration have often been taken as evidence for minstrel composition, evidence, that is, of a native, popular tradition. Nonetheless, the effects achieved by Minot in "The Battle of Bannockburn," for instance, which combines an incremental refrain "wele wurth the while . . . for thai er ful of gile," with iteration between the fourth and fifth line of each stanza and concatenation between each stanza, are not less practiced, less decorative or less artful than are the devices of "equivoque" and "retrograde" employed by Machaut in the ballade "Douce dame, vo maniere jolie," in which the final word in the line provides a syllable for the first word in the succeeding line:

Douce dame, vo maniere jolie
Lie en amours mon cuer et mon desir
Desiramment, si que, sans tricherie,

Introduction

Chierie adès en serez, sans partir.
Partir vaut miex que d'autre souvenir
Venir peüst en moy, qui en ardure
Durement vif et humblement l'endure.

Dure à moy seul, de tous biens assevie,
Vie d'onneur plaisant à maintenir
Tenir m'estuet dou tout en vo baillie
Liement, et, pour joie desservir,
Servir vous vueil et mes maus conjoir.
Joïr n'espoir, helas! et sans laidure
Durement vif et humblement l'endure.

[Sweet lady, your pretty ways bind in love my heart and my desire desiringly, so that you will always be held dear for them without trickery, completely. (Even) parting is worth more than the thought of another can produce in me, who while burning live painfully and endure it humbly.

Hard to me alone, lady replete with all good, I must lead a life of honour happily, pleasant to maintain, wholly in your power, and to merit joy I wish to serve you and with you take pleasure in my sufferings. I have no hope of having joy, alas! and without offending, I live painfully and endure it humbly.]
    (Wimsatt, pp. 16–17)

Certain of these characteristics can of course be paralleled elsewhere in what may be termed clerkly or "art" poetry in Latin:

Petre, piis plausibus pro petra punito,
Plaudat præsens populus pectore polito;
Petrus pater pauperum purus prædicator
Petram plebi prædicat pacis propagator. . . .
    (Wright and Halliwell, II, 20)

[Peter, with purified hearts the people here give reverent praise for the Rock once slain. Father to the poor, spotless preacher, sower of peace — Peter proclaims the Rock to the people.]

Or in Anglo-Norman, "The Wisdom of Lady Desmonia," for instance:

Soule su, simple, e saunz solas,
    seignury me somount sojouner;
Si suppris sei de moun solas,
    sages se deit soul solacer.
    (Wright and Halliwell, II, 256)

[Should I suffer alone, free and without solace, his lordship bids me to remain. When I am deprived of my solace, wisdom itself teaches the solace of solitude.]

Or in English as well:

> Love havith me broght in lither thoght.
> thoght ic ab to blinne:
> blinne to thench hit is for noght;
> Noght is love of sinne.
>   Sinne me havith in care ibroght.
> broght in mochil un-winne:
> Winne to weld ic had i-thoght
> Thoght is that ic am inne.
>   In me is care. how i ssal fare
> fare ic wol and funde.
> Fare ic with outen are
> ar i be broght to grunde.
>   (Furnivall, pp. 22–23)

This is not to argue, of course, that Minot is imitating French courtly verse — the fervid nationalism which leads him to assail those Scots who affect French manners, "Ful few find ye yowre frende / For all yowre Frankis fare" (6.19–20) would, one suspects, engender a similar opinion regarding French lyric poetry. Some critics link Minot's verse with the rudimentary alliterative line to be found, for instance, in the monorhymed quatrains of MS Harley 2253, "Of rybaudz y ryme ant rede o my rolle," or in Richard Rolle's *Ego dormio*, "Robes and ritches rotes in dike / Prowde payntyng slakes into sorrow" (Pickering, p. 178), but it is the alliterative Harley lyrics, with their concatenation, iteration, complex stanza forms, and alliteration of stressed syllables — techniques quite different from those of Machaut and Deschamps, as Wimsatt has shown (p. 45) — whose prosody seems closest to Minot's. These are techiques also shared with a constellation of longer narrative poems like *The Pistel of Swete Susan* and some of the York plays — poems which share with Minot a common fund of alliterative collocations. Minot's stylistic range is limited and its effects are largely decorative. When Chaucer turns to write battle poetry, as in the Knight's Tale, however, one hears in the sudden density of alliteration and monosyllabic rhymes the echoes of that tradition of war songs within which Minot works.

Introduction

Select Bibliography

Manuscript

Cotton Galba E.ix

Critical Editions

Collette, Carolyn P., ed. *The Poems of Laurence Minot*. University of Massachusetts Ph.D. Dissertation, 1971.

Emerson, Oliver Farrar, ed. *A Middle English Reader*. London: MacMillan, 1927. Pp. 157–65.

Hall, Joseph, ed. *The Poems of Laurence Minot*. 3rd ed. Oxford: Clarendon, 1914.

James, Thomas Beaumont, and John Simons, eds. *The Poems of Laurence Minot: 1333–1352*. Exeter: University of Exeter Press, 1989.

Ritson, Joseph, ed. *Poems written anno MCCCLII. By Laurence Minot*. With Introductory Dissertations on the Scotish Wars of Edward III by Joseph Ritson. London: J. H. Burn, 1825.

Robbins, Rossell Hope, ed. *Historical Poems of the XIV and XV Centuries*. New York: Columbia University Press, 1959. Pp. 30–39.

Scholle, Wilhelm, ed. *Laurence Minots Lieder mit Grammatisch-Metrischer Einleitung*. Quellen und Forschungen zur Sprach- und Culturgeschichte der Germanischen Völker. Strassburg and London: Karl J. Trübner, 1884.

Sisam, Kenneth, ed. *Fourteenth Century Verse and Prose*. Oxford: Clarendon, 1975. Pp. 152–56.

Stedman, Douglas C., ed. *The War Ballads of Laurence Minot*. Dublin: Hodges, Figgis & Co., 1917.

Wright, Thomas, ed. *Political Poems and Songs Relating to English History*. Vol. 1. London: Longman, 1859. Pp. 58–91.

———, ed. *The Political Songs of England from the Reign of John to that of Edward II*. London: Printed for the Camden Society by John Bowyer Nichols and Son, 1839.

Related Studies

Allmand, C. T., ed. *Society at War: The Experience of England and France During the Hundred Years War*. Edinburgh: Oliver & Boyd, 1973.

———. *The Hundred Years War: England and France at War c. 1300–c. 1450*. Cambridge: Cambridge University Press, 1988.

Baird, Ian F., ed. *Scotish Feilde and Flodden Feilde: Two Flodden Poems*. New York: Garland, 1982.

Barnie, John. *War in Medieval English Society: Social Values in the Hundred Years War 1337–99*. Ithaca: Cornell University Press, 1974.

Beadle, Richard. *The York Plays*. London: E. Arnold, 1982.

Bennett, Michael J. *Community, Class and Careerism: Cheshire and Lancashire Society in the Age of* Sir Gawain and the Green Knight. Cambridge: Cambridge University Press, 1983.

Benson, Larry D., and Edward E. Foster. *King Arthur's Death: The Middle English Stanzaic Morte Arthur and Alliterative Morte Arthure*. Kalamazoo: Medieval Institute Publications, 1994.

Boffey, Julia, and John J. Thompson. "Anthologies and Miscellanies: Production and Choice of Texts." In *Book Production and Publishing in Britain 1375–1475*. Ed. Jeremy Griffiths and Derek Pearsall. Cambridge and New York: Cambridge University Press, 1989. Pp. 279–315.

Brook, G. L., ed. *The Harley Lyrics: The Middle English Lyrics of MS. Harley 2253*. Manchester: Manchester University Press, 1948.

Brown, Arthur C. L. "On the Origin of Stanza-linking in English Alliterative Verse." *The Romanic Review* 7.3 (1916), 271–83.

Cable, Thomas. "Middle English Meter and Its Theoretical Implications." *The Yearbook of Langland Studies* 2 (1988), 47–69.

Coldewey, John C., ed. *Early English Drama: An Anthology*. New York: Garland, 1993.

Doyle, A. I. "The Manuscripts." In *Middle English Alliterative Poetry and Its Literary Background*. Ed. David Lawton. Cambridge: D. S. Brewer, 1982. Pp. 88–100.

Duggan, Hoyt. "The Shape of the B-Verse in Middle English Alliterative Poetry." *Speculum* 61.3 (1986), 564–92.

Ellis, Henry. *Original Letters Illustrative of English History*, 1st Series, Vol. 1. New York: AMS Press, 1970.

Fifield, M. J. *Alliteration in the Middle English Lyrics*. University of Illinois Ph.D. Dissertation, 1960.

Finlayson, John. *"Morte Arthure*: The Date and a Source for the Contemporary References." *Speculum* 42.4 (1967), 624–38.

Francis, A. D. *The Wine Trade*. London: Adam & Charles Block, 1972.

Froissart, Sir John. *The Chronicles of England, France and Spain*. Trans. Thomas Johnes; condensed by H. P. Dunster. New York: E. P. Dutton, 1961.

Furnivall, Frederick J. *Early English Poems and Lives of Saints*. Transactions of the Philological Society. Vol. 11. Berlin: A. Asher & Co., 1862.

Hingeston, Francis C., ed. *Royal and Historical Letters*, R.S. 18. 2 vols. London: Longman, Green, Longman, and Roberts, 1860.

Hulme, William Henry, ed. *The Middle English Harrowing of Hell and Gospel of Nicodemus*. Early English Text Society, e.s. 100. London: Oxford University Press, 1907; rpt. 1961.

Johnston, Alexandra F., and Margaret Rogerson, eds. *Records of Early English Drama: York*. 2 vols. Toronto: University of Toronto Press, 1979.

Kane, George. "Some Fourteenth-Century 'Political' Poems." In *Medieval English Religious and Ethical Literature*. Eds. Gregory Kratzmann and James Simpson. Cambridge: D. S. Brewer, 1986. Pp. 82–91.

Keiser, George R. "Edward III and the *Alliterative Morte Arthure*." *Speculum* 48.4 (1973), 37–51.

Kendrick, Laura. "On Reading Medieval Political Verse: Two Partisan Poems from the Reign of Edward II." *Mediaevalia: A Journal of Medieval Studies* 5 (1979), 183–204.

Lawler, Traugott, ed. and trans. *The Parisiana Poetria of John of Garland*. Yale Studies in English, 182. New Haven: Yale University Press, 1974.

Lawton, David. *Middle English Alliterative Poetry and Its Literary Background*. Cambridge: D. S. Brewer, 1982.

Luttrell, C. A. "Three North-West Midland Manuscripts." *Neophilologus* 42 (1958), 38–50.

McKisack, May. *The Fourteenth Century: 1307–1399*. Oxford: Clarendon Press, 1959.

Medary, Margaret P. "Stanza-Linking in Middle English Verse." *The Romanic Review* 7 (1916), 243–70.

Moore, Samuel. "Lawrence Minot." *Modern Language Notes* 35 (1920), 78–81.

Neillands, Robin. *The Hundred Years War*. London: Guild; New York: Routledge, 1990.

Oakden, J. P. *Alliterative Poetry in Middle English*. 2 vols. Manchester: Manchester University Press, 1930; 1935.

Oman, Charles. *A History of the Art of War in the Middle Ages*. Vol. 2: 1278–1485. New York: Houghton Mifflin Company, 1924.

Ormrod, W. M. *The Reign of Edward III: Crown and Political Society in England, 1327–1377*. New Haven: Yale University Press, 1990.

Osberg, Richard. "The Jesse Tree in the 1432 London Entry of Henry VI: Messianic Kingship and the Rule of Justice." *The Journal of Medieval and Renaissance Studies* 16 (1986), 213–32.

———. "Alliterative Technique in the Lyrics of MS Harley 2253." *Modern Philology* 82.2 (1984), 125–55.

Packe, Michael. *King Edward III*. Ed. L. C. B. Seaman. London and Boston: Routledge & Kegan Paul, 1983.

Parker, Roscoe E. "Laurence Minot's Tribute to John Badding." *PMLA* 37.2 (1922), 360–65.

Partridge, A. C. *A Companion to Old and Middle English Studies*. Totowa, N.J.: Barnes and Noble, 1982.

Pearsall, Derek. *The Life of Geoffrey Chaucer*. Oxford and Cambridge, Mass.: Blackwell, 1992.

———, ed. *Manuscripts and Readers in Fifteenth-Century England: The Literary Implications of Manuscript Study*. Cambridge: D. S. Brewer, 1983.

———. *Old English and Middle English Poetry*. London and Boston: Routledge & Kegan Paul, 1977.

Pickering, O. S. "Newly Discovered Secular Lyrics from Later Thirteenth-Century Cheshire." *The Review of English Studies* 43 (1992), 157–80.

Piers Plowman. Ed. W. W. Skeat. *EETS* o.s. 38. London: Oxford University Press, 1869.

The Riverside Chaucer. Gen. ed. Larry D. Benson. Boston: Houghton Mifflin, 1987.

Robbins, Rossell Hope. "A Gawain Epigone." *Modern Language Notes* 58 (1943), 361–66.

———. "The Poems of Humphrey Newton Esq., 1466–1536." *PMLA* 65 (1950), 249–81.

Scattergood, V. J. *Politics and Poetry in the Fifteenth Century*. New York: Barnes and Noble, 1971.

Taylor, Rupert. *The Political Prophecy in England*. New York: Columbia University Press, 1911.

Thompson, John J. *Robert Thornton and the London Thornton Manuscript: British Library MS Additional 31042*. Cambridge: D. S. Brewer, 1987.

Turville-Petre, Thorlac. "Some Medieval English Manuscripts in the North-East Midlands." In *Manuscripts and Readers in Fifteenth-Century England: The Literary Implications of Manuscript Study*. Ed. Derek Pearsall. Cambridge: D. S. Brewer, 1983. Pp. 125–41.

——. "The Lament for Sir John Berkeley." *Speculum* 57.2 (1982), 332–39.

Vale, Juliet. *Edward III and Chivalry: Chivalric Society and its Context 1270–1350*. Woodbridge: Boydell Press, 1982.

Wimsatt, James I. *Chaucer and his French Contemporaries: Natural Music in the Fourteenth Century*. Toronto: University of Toronto Press, 1991.

Wright, Thomas, ed. *Political Songs of England from the Reign of John to that of Edward II*. Camden Society, vol. 6. London: J. B. Nichols and Son, 1839.

—— and James Orchard Halliwell. *Reliquiae antiquae*. 2 vols. London: William Pickering, 1843.

Wynnere and Wastoure and The Parlement of the Thre Ages. Ed. Warren Ginsberg. Kalamazoo: Medieval Institute Publications, 1992.

Year Books of the Reign of King Edward the Third, Year XIX. 15 vols. Ed. and trans. Luke Owen Pike. R.S. 31, vol. 13. London: Longman and Co., 1906.

Bibliography

Robbins, Rossell Hope. "XIII. Poems Dealing with Contemporary Conditions." In *A Manual of the Writings in Middle English 1050–1500*. Gen. ed. Albert E. Hartung. Vol. 5. New Haven: The Connecticut Academy of Arts and Sciences, 1975. Pp. 1412–16; 1657–61.

The Poems of Laurence Minot

[I]   **Lithes and I sall tell yow tyll**   [f. 52a¹]
        the bataile of Halidon Hyll.

        Trew king that sittes in trone,   *[God]*
        unto The I tell my tale,
        and unto The I bid a bone,   *prayer*
        for Thou ert bute of all my bale.   *remedy; grief*
5   Als Thou made midelerd and the mone   *earth; moon*
        and bestes and fowles grete and smale,
        unto me send Thi socore sone
        and dresce my dedes in this dale.   *guide*

        In this dale I droupe and dare   *I am downcast and dismayed*
10   for dern dedes that done me dere;   *secret; cause me injury*
        of Ingland had my hert grete care
        when Edward founded first to were.   *prepared to go; war*
        The Franche men war frek to fare   *eager*
        ogaines him with scheld and spere;   *against*
15   thai turned ogayn with sides sare
        and al thaire pomp noght worth a pere.   *pear*

        A pere of prise es more sum tyde   *value; time*
        than all the boste of Normondye.   *boast*
        Thai sent thaire schippes on ilka side   *every*
20   with flesch and wine and whete and rye.   *meat*
        With hert and hand es noght at hide   *is no need to conceal*
        forto help Scotland gan thai hye;   *did they hasten*
        thai fled and durst no dede habide   *dared; action; await*
        and all thaire fare noght wurth a flye.   *vaunting*

25   For all thaire fare thai durst noght fight,
        for dedes dint had thai slike dout;   *Of death's blow they had such fear*

33

of Scotland had thai never sight
ay whils thai war of wordes stout.   *although; boastful*
Thai wald have mend tham at thaire might   *demeaned*
30 and besy war thai thareobout.
Now God help Edward in his right —
Amen! — and all his redy rowt.

His redy rout mot Jhesu spede
and save tham both by night and day;
35 that lord of hevyn mot Edward lede   *must; favor*
and maintene him als he wele may.
The Scottes now all wide will sprede,
for thai have failed of thaire pray.   *their prey*
Now er thai dareand all for drede   *are; dispirited; terror*
40 that war bifore so stout and gay.   *who were*

Gai thai war, and wele thai thoght
on the Erle Morré and other ma.   *others as well (more)*
Thai said it suld ful dere be boght   *should*
the land that thai war flemid fra.   *were exiled from*
45 Philip Valays wordes wroght   *contrived*
and said he suld thaire enmys sla,
bot all thaire wordes was for noght —   [f. 52a²
thai mun be met if thai war ma.   *must; more*

Ma manasinges yit have thai maked —   *More menaces yet*
50 mawgre mot thai have to mede! —   *shame; reward*
and many nightes als have thai waked
to dere all Ingland with thaire dede.   *injure*
Bot, loved be God, the pride es slaked   *diminished*
of tham that war so stout on stede,   *place*
55 and sum of tham es levid all naked   *are left*
noght fer fro Berwik opon Twede.   *not far from*

A litell fro that forsaid toune,
Halydon Hill that es the name,
thare was crakked many a crowne
60 of wild Scottes and alls of tame.   *also*
Thare was thaire baner born all doune;

34

Poem I

to mak slike boste thai war to blame,   *such boast*
bot never the les ay er thai boune   *always they are prepared*
to wait Ingland with sorow and schame.   *to inflict injury on England*

65   Shame thai have als I here say;
at Dondé now es done thaire daunce,   *(see note)*
and wend thai most another way,   *go*
evyn thurgh Flandres into France.
On Filip Valas fast cri thai
70   thare for to dwell and him avaunce,
and no thing list tham than of play   *pleased them; pleasure*
sen tham es tide this sary chance.   *since; has befallen*

This sary chaunce tham es bitid,
for thai war fals and wonder fell,   *cruel*
75   for cursed caitefes er thai kid   *wretches; known*
and ful of treson, suth to tell.   *truth*
Sir Jon the Comyn had thai hid;
in haly kirk thai did him quell,   *kill*
and tharfore many a Skottis brid   *woman*
80   with dole er dight that thai most dwell.   *grief; destined; suffer*

Thare dwelled oure king, the suth to saine,   *truth; say*
with his menye a litell while;   *retinue*
he gaf gude confort on that plaine
to all his men obout a myle.
85   All if his men war mekill of maine,   *great of might*
ever thai douted tham of gile;
the Scottes gaudes might no thing gain   *tricks*
for all thai stumbilde at that stile.   *stumbled at those steps*

Thus in that stowre thai left thaire live   *conflict; their lives*
90   that war bifore so proud in prese.   *crowd of battle*
Jhesu for Thi woundes five
in Ingland help us to have pese.   *peace*

[II]   **Now for to tell yow will I turn**
         of the batayl of Banocburn.

    Skottes out of Berwik and of Abirdene,   [f. 52b[1]
    at the Bannok burn war ye to kene!   *stream; too bold*
    Thare slogh ye many sakles, als it was sene,   *innocent, as*
    and now has king Edward wroken it I wene: *avenged; believe*
5   it es wrokin I wene, wele wurth the while;   *happy be the occasion*
      war yit with the Skottes, for thai er ful of gile.   *wary*

    Whare er ye, Skottes of Saint Johnes toune?
    The boste of yowre baner es betin all doune;
    when ye bosting will bede, sir Edward es boune   *offer; ready*
10   for to kindel yow care and crak yowre crowne:
      he has crakked yowre croune, wele worth the while;
      schame bityde the Skottes, for thai er full of gile.

    Skottes of Striflin war steren and stout;   *Sterling; stern*
    of God ne of gude men had thai no dout.
15   Now have thai, the pelers, priked obout,   *thieves, spurred*
    bot at the last sir Edward rifild thair rout: *despoiled their company*
      he has rifild thaire rout, wele wurth the while,
      bot ever er thai under, bot gaudes and gile.   *defeated; pretense; deceit*

    Rughfute riveling, now kindels thi care,   *Rough-shod raw-hide boot*
20   berebag with thi boste, thi biging es bare;   *bag carrier; house*
    fals wretche and forsworn, whider wiltou fare?   *where will you go*
    Busk the unto Brig and abide thare: *Hurry; Bruges*
      thare wretche saltou won and wery the while;   *shall you live; curse*
      thi dwelling in Dondé es done for thi gile.   *Dundee*

25   The Skotte gase in Burghes and betes the stretes,   *pounds the pavements*
    all thise Inglis men harmes he hetes;   *vows*
    fast makes he his mone to men that he metes,
    bot fone frendes he findes that his bale betes: *few; anguish relieves*
      fune betes his bale, wele wurth the while;   *few*
30   he uses all threting with gaudes and gile.

Poem II

Bot many man thretes and spekes ful ill
that sum tyme war better to be stane still.   *utterly (stone)*
The Skot in his wordes has wind for to spill,
for at the last Edward sall have al his will:
35   he had his will at Berwik, wele wurth the while;
     Skottes broght him the kayes, bot get for thaire gile.   *keys; watch out for*

[III]   **How Edward the king come in Braband**
        and toke homage of all the land.

God that schope both se and sand *created; sea*
save Edward king of Ingland,
both body, saul, and life
and grante him joy withowten strif.
5   For mani men to him er wroth *because of him are*
in Fraunce and in Flandres both,
for he defendes fast his right;
and tharto Jhesu grante him might
and so to do both night and day
10 that yt may be to Goddes pay. *pleasure*

Oure king was cumen, trewly to tell, [f. 52b²
into Brabant for to dwell.
The kayser Lowis of Bavere,
that in that land than had no pere, *no equal*
15 he and als his sons two *also*
and other princes many mo —
bisschoppes and prelates war thare fele *many*
that had ful mekill werldly wele, *great worldly success*
princes and pople ald and yong,
20 al that spac with Duche tung — *German*
all thai come with grete honowre
sir Edward to save and socoure
and proferd him with all thayre rede *advice*
for to hald the kinges stede.

25 The duke of Braband first of all
swore for thing that might bifall *swore that no matter what befell*
that he suld both day and night
help sir Edward in his right
in toun, in feld, in frith and fen. *woods; marshland*
30 This swore the duke and all his men
and al the lordes that with him lend, *remained*
and tharto held thai up thaire hend.
Than king Edward toke his rest
at Andwerp whare him liked best,

38

35	and thare he made his moné playne	*money evident*
	that no man suld say thare ogayne,	
	his moné that was gude and lele	*money; loyal*
	left in Braband ful mekill dele,	*great portion*
	and all that land untill this day	
40	fars the better for that jornay.	
	When Philip the Valas herd of this,	
	tharat he was full wroth I wis.	
	He gert assemble his barounes,	*caused to*
	princes and lordes of many tounes;	
45	at Pariss toke thai thaire counsaile	
	whilk pointes might tham moste availe,	*which goal*
	and in all wise thai tham bithoght	
	to stroy Ingland and bring to noght.	
	Schipmen sone war efter sent	
50	to here the kinges cumandment,	*hear*
	and the galaies men also	*galley*
	that wist both of wele and wo.	*knew both victory and defeat*
	He cumand than that men suld fare	
	till Ingland and for no thing spare	
55	bot brin and sla both man and wife	*burn; slay*
	and childe, that none suld pas with life.	*should escape*
	The galay men held up thaire handes	*galley*
	and thanked God of thir tithandes.	*tidings*
	At Hamton, als I understand,	*Southampton* [f53a[1]
60	come the gaylayes unto land,	
	and ful fast thai slogh and brend,	
	bot noght so mekill als sum men wend.	*much; intended*
	For, or thai wened, war thai mett	*before they knew*
	with men that sone thaire laykes lett.	*halted their games*
65	Sum was knokked on the hevyd	*head*
	that the body thare bilevid;	*remained*
	sum lay stareand on the sternes,	*stars*
	and sum lay knoked out thair hernes.	*brains*
	Than with tham was none other gle	*merry-making*
70	bot ful fain war thai that might fle.	*full glad were*

The galay men the suth to say · *truth*
most nedes turn another way;
thai soght the stremis fer and wide · *waterways far*
in Flandres and in Seland syde.
75 Than saw thai whare Cristofer stode · *(see note)*
at Armouth opon the flude. · *Yarmouth; sea*
Than went thai theder all bidene, · *together*
the galayes men with hertes kene, · *bold hearts*
eight and forty galays and mo,
80 and with tham als war tarettes two · *two supply ships*
and other many of galiotes · *small galleys*
with grete noumber of smale botes.
All thai hoved on the flode · *intended; sea*
to stele sir Edward mens gode. · *steal*

85 Edward oure king than was noght there,
bot sone when it come to his ere · *ear*
he sembled all his men full still
and said to tham what was his will.
Ilk man made him redy then; · *Each*
90 so went the king and all his men
unto thaire schippes ful hastily
als men that war in dede doghty. · *indeed brave*

Thai fand the galay men grete wane, · *plenty*
a hundereth ever ogaynes ane. · *against one*
95 The Inglis men put tham to were
ful baldly with bow and spere;
thai slogh thare of the galaies men
ever sexty ogaynes ten,
that sum ligges yit in that mire
100 all hevidles with owten hire. · *beheaded; pay*

The Inglis men war armed wele
both in yren and in stele.
Thai faght ful fast both day and night,
als lang als tham lasted might,
105 bot galay men war so many
that Inglis men wex all wery. · *became exhausted*

Poem III

Help thai soght, bot thare come nane; [f.53a²]

than unto God thai made thaire mane. *their complaint (moan)*

Bot sen the time that God was born, *since*

110 ne a hundreth yere biforn,

war never men better in fight

than Ingliss men whils thai had myght. *strength*

Bot sone all maistri gan thai mis — *But soon they lost the upper hand*

God bring thaire saules untill his blis,

115 and God assoyl tham of thaire sin *absolve*

for the gude will that thai war in. Amen.

Listens now and leves me. *believe*

Who so lifes, thai sall se

that it mun be ful dere boght

120 that thir galay men have wroght.

Thai hoved still opon the flode

and reved pouer men thaire gude. *robbed*

Thai robbed and did mekill schame

and ay bare Inglis men the blame.

125 Now Jhesus save all Ingland

and blis it with his haly hand. Amen.

[IV] Edward oure cumly king
  in Braband has his woning   *dwelling*
  with mani cumly knight.   *handsome*
  And in that land, trewly to tell,
5 ordanis he still for to dwell,
  to time he think to fight.

  Now God that es of mightes maste   *greatest power*
  grant him grace of the Haly Gaste
  his heritage to win.
10 And Mari moder of mercy fre,
  save oure king and his menye   *retinue*
  fro sorow and schame and syn.   *from*

  Thus in Braband has he bene,
  whare he bifore was seldom sene,
15 for to prove thaire japes.   *test; deceit*
  Now no langer wil he spare,
  bot unto Fraunce fast will he fare
  to confort him with grapes.

  Furth he ferd into France —   *went*
20 God save him fro mischance
  and all his cumpany.
  The nobill duc of Braband
  with him went into that land,
  redy to lif or dy.   *live; die*

25 Than the riche floure de lice   *fleur de lys (lily flower)*
  wan thare ful litill prise;   *fame*
  fast he fled for ferde.   *fear*
  The right aire of that cuntré   *heir*
  es cumen with all his knightes fre   [f. 53b¹
30 to schac him by the berd.   *to make him tremble with fear*

  Sir Philip the Valayse,
  wit his men in tho dayes,   *with*
  to batale had he thoght.
  He bad his men tham purvay   *provision themselves*

35   with owten lenger delay,
       bot he ne held it noght.

       He broght folk ful grete wone,   *abundance*
       ay sevyn oganis one,   *even; against*
       that ful wele wapnid were.   *armed*
40   Bot sone when he herd ascry   *a report*
       that king Edward was nere tharby,
       than durst he noght cum nere.   *dared*

       In that mornig fell a myst,
       and when oure Ingliss men it wist,   *knew*
45   it changed all thaire chere.   *their mood*
       Oure king unto God made his bone,   *prayer*
       and God sent him gude confort sone —
       the weder wex ful clere.   *became*

       Oure king and his men held the felde
50   stalwortly with spere and schelde,
       and thoght to win his right,
       with lordes and with knightes kene
       and other doghty men bydene   *together*
       that war ful frek to fight.   *very eager*

55   When sir Philip of France herd tell
       that king Edward in feld walld dwell,   *would*
       than gayned him no gle.   *pleasure*
       He traisted of no better bote,   *expected; remedy*
       bot both on hors and on fote
60   he hasted him to fle.

       It semid he was ferd for strokes
       when he did fell his grete okes
       obout his pavilyoune.
       Abated was than all his pride,
65   for langer thare durst he noght bide —
       his bost was broght all doune.

The king of Beme had cares colde, *Bohemia; vexing anxieties*
that was ful hardy and bolde,
a stede to umstride. *steed; ride*
70 The king als of Naverne *Navarre*
war faire feld in the ferene *lay low in the bracken*
thaire heviddes for to hide. *heads*

And leves wele, it es no lye, *believe*
the felde hat Flemangrye *(see note)*
75 that king Edward was in,
with princes that war stif ande bolde
and dukes that war doghty tolde *esteemed* [f. 53b²
in batayle to bigin.

The princes that war riche on raw *princes that were splendid in battle order*
80 gert nakers strike and trumpes blaw *had drums*
and made mirth at thaire might.
Both alblast and many a bow *crossbow*
war redy railed opon a row *ordered*
and ful frek for to fight. *keen*

85 Gladly thai gaf mete and drink
so that thai suld the better swink *work*
the wight men that thar ware. *stout*
Sir Philip of Fraunce fled for dout *fear*
and hied him hame with all his rout —
90 coward! God giff him care.

For thare than had the lely flowre
lorn all halely his honowre, *completely lost its*
that sogat fled for ferd. *thus; fear*
Bot oure king Edward come ful still,
95 when that he trowed no harm him till *believed*
and keped him in the berde. *confronted him in combat (opposed him face to face)*

Poem V

[V]   **Lithes and the batail I sal bigyn**
        of Inglisch men & Normandes in the Swyn

     Minot with mowth had menid to make   *intended*
     suth sawes and sad for sum mens sake.   *serious*
     The wordes of sir Edward makes me to wake;
     wald he salue us sone mi sorow suld slake.   *greet*
5   War mi sorow slaked, sune wald I sing,
       when God will sir Edward sal us bute bring.   *remedy*

     Sir Philip the Valas cast was in care
     and said sir Hugh Kyret to Flandres suld fare,
     and have Normondes inogh to leve on his lare   *believe; lesson*
10   all Flandres to brin and mak it all bare.   *burn*
     Bot, unkind coward, wo was him thare;
     when he sailed in the Swin, it sowed him sare.   *pained; sorely*
       Sare it tham smerted that ferd out of France;
       thare lered Inglis men tham a new daunce.   *taught*

15   The buriase of Bruge ne war noght to blame;   *townsmen*
     I pray Jhesu save tham fro sin and fro schame,
     for thai war sone at the Sluse all by a name,
     whare many of the Normandes tok mekill grame.   *great harm*

     When Bruges and Ipyre hereof herd tell,
20   thai sent Edward to wit, that was in Arwell;
     than had he no liking langer to dwell.
     He hasted him to the Swin with sergantes snell,   *soldiers quick*
     to mete with the Normandes, that fals war and fell,
     that had ment if thai might al Flandres to quell.

25   King Edward unto sail was ful sune dight,   *soon prepared*
     with erles and barons and many kene knight.
     Thai come byfor Blankebergh on Saint Jons night —   [f. 54a[1]
     that was to the Normondes a well sary sight.
     Yit trumped thai and daunced with torches ful bright;
30   in the wilde waniand was thaire hertes light.   *waning [of the moon]*

Opon the morn efter, if I suth say,
a meri man, sir Robard out of Morlay,
at half eb in the Swin soght he the way.   *ebb tide*
Thare lered men the Normandes at bukler to play   *men taught; sword and shield*
35   helpid tham no prayer that thai might pray —
the wreches es wonnen; thaire wapin es oway.   *captured; destroyed*

The erle of Norhamton helpid at that nede
als wise man of wordes and worthli in wede.
Sir Walter the Mawnay, God gif him mede,   *reward*
40   was bold of body in batayl to bede.   *present himself*

The duc of Lankaster was dight for to drive,   *ready; pursue*
with mani mody man that thoght for to thrive.   *courageous*
Wele and stalworthly stint he that strive   *stopped*
that few of the Normandes left thai olive.
45   Fone left thai olive bot did tham to lepe;   *Few; alive; caused him*
      men may find by the flode a hundred on hepe.

Sir Wiliam of Klinton was eth for to knaw;   *easy*
mani stout bachilere broght he on raw —   *line*
it semid with thaire schoting als it war snaw.   *archery; snow*
50   The bost of the Normandes broght thai ful law.
      Thaire bost was abated and thaire mekil pride;
      fer might thai noght fle bot thare bud tham bide.

The gude erle of Glowceter, God mot him glade,
broght many boldmen with bowes ful brade;   *quite large*
55   to biker with the Normandes baldely thai bade   *fight; offered*
and in middes the flode did tham to wade.
      To wade war tho wretches casten in the brim;
      the kaitefs come out of France at lere tham to swim.   *to teach*

I prays John Badding als one of the best;
60   faire come he sayland out of the suthwest.
To prove of tha Normandes was he ful prest;   *ready*
till he had foghten his fill he had never rest.

Poem V

John of Aile of the Sluys with scheltron ful schene — *squadron; bright*
was comen into Cagent cantly and kene. — *boldly*
65 Bot sone was his trumping turned to tene; — *sorrow*
of him had sir Edward his will als I wene.

The schipmen of Ingland sailed ful swith — *quickly*
that none of the Normandes fro tham might skrith. — *escape*
Who so kouth wele his craft thare might it kith; — *know*
70 of al the gude that thai gat gaf thai no tithe.

Two hundreth and mo schippes on the sandes
had oure Inglis men won with thaire handes.
The kogges of Ingland war broght out of bandes — *ships; bonds*
and also the Cristofir that in the streme standes.
75   In that stound thai stode with stremers ful still, — [f. 54a²
   till thai wist full wele sir Edwardes will.

Sir Edward oure gude king wurthi in wall — *choice of persons*
faght wele on that flude — faire mot him fall! — *may good fortune befall him*
Als it es custom of king to confort tham all,
80 so thanked he gudely the grete and the small.
   He thanked tham gudely, God gif him mede; — *reward*
   thus come oure king in the Swin till that gude dede.

This was the bataile that fell in the Swin
whare many Normandes made mekill din.
85 Wele war thai armed up to the chin,
   bot God and sir Edward gert thaire boste blin. — *made their boast cease*
   Thus blinned thaire boste als we wele ken; — *know*
   God assoyle thaire sawls sais all. Amen. — *absolve*

[VI]   **Herkins how king Edward lay**
         with his men bifor Tournay.

Towrenay, yow has tight   *determined*
    to timber trey and tene.   *to build affliction and sorrow*
A bore with brenis bright   *boar; shining coats of mail (see note)*
    es broght opon yowre grene.
5   That es a semely sight,   *handsome*
    with schilterouns faire and schene.   *squadrons; bright*
Thi domes day es dight,   *judgment; appointed*
    bot thou be war, I wene.   *advise*

When all yowre wele es went,   *joy is gone*
10   yowre wo wakkins ful wide.   *woe awakens*
To sighing er ye sent,
    with sorow on ilka syde.   *every*
Ful rewfull es yowre rent;   *pitiable; income*
    all redles may ye ride.   *unadvised*
15 The harmes that ye have hent   *have seized you*
    now may ye hele and hide.   *conceal*

Hides and helis als hende,   *quickly*
    for ye er cast in care.
Ful few find ye yowre frende,
20   for all yowre Frankis fare.   *French manners*
Sir Philip sall yow schende —   *ruin*
    whi leve ye at his lare?   *believe; teaching*
No bowes now thar yow bende;
    of blis ye er all bare.   *barren*

25 All bare er ye of blis;
    no bost may be yowre bote.   *reward*
All mirthes mun ye mis;   *must*
    oure men sall with yow mote.   *litigate*
Who sall yow clip and kys   *embrace*
30   and fall yowre folk to fote?   *to whose feet shall your people fall*
A were es wroght, I wis,
    yowre walles with to wrote.   *root up*

Wrote thai sal yowre dene,   *Uproot; refuge* [f. 54b[1]
   of dintes ye may yow dowte.   *With blows*
35   Yowre biginges sall men brene   *dwellings; burn*
   and breke yowre walles obout.
Ful redles may ye ren   *In confusion (disarray); run*
   with all yowre rewful rout.   *retinue*
With care men sall yow ken   *advise*
40   Edward yowre lord to lout.   *bow down to*

To lout yowre lord in land
   with list men sall yow lere.   *by skillful; be taught*
Yowre harmes cumes at hand,
   als ye sall hastly here.
45   Now frendschip suld ye fande
   of sir Philip yowre fere   *companion*
to bring yow out of band   *feudal bonds*
   or ye be broght on bere.   *before; bier*

On bere when ye er broght,
50   than cumes Philip to late.
He hetes and haldes yow noght;   *promises*
   with hert ye may him hate.
A bare now has him soght   *boar*
   till Turnay the right gate,   *way*
55   that es ful wele bithoght
   to stop Philip the strate   *narrow way*
     ful still.
   Philip was fain he moght   *glad; must*
   graunt sir Edward his will.

60   If ye will trow my tale,   *believe*
   A duke tuke leve that tide.
A Braban brewed that bale;   *woe*
   he bad no langer bide.
Giftes grete and smale
65   war sent him on his side.
Gold gert all that gale   *occasioned; course of action*
   and made him rapely ride   *quickly*
     till dede.   *to his death*

In hert he was unhale; *unwholesome*
70   he come thare moste for mede. *reward*

King Edward, frely fode, *noble man*
  in Fraunce he will noght blin *cease*
to mak his famen wode *enemies mad*
  that er wonand thare in. *are living*
75 God, that rest on Rode *Cross*
  for sake of Adams syn,
strenkith him main and mode *strengthen; body and spirit*
  his reght in France to win *royal perogative*
    and have.
80 God grante him graces gode
  and fro all sins us save. Amen.

Poem VII

[VII]	**How Edward at Hogges unto land wan**	
	and rade thurgh France or ever he blan.	*before; stopped*

	Men may rede in romance right	[f. 54b²
	of a grete clerk that Merlin hight;	*is named*
	ful many bokes er of him wreten,	
	als thir clerkes wele may witten,	*know*
5	and yit in many privé nokes	*private corners*
	may men find of Merlin bokes.	
	Merlin said thus with his mowth:	
	Out of the north into the sowth	
	suld cum a bare over the se	*boar*
10	that suld mak many man to fle.	
	And in the se, he said ful right,	
	suld he schew ful mekill might,	*great*
	and in France he suld bigin	
	to mak tham wrath that er tharein.	*angry*
15	Untill the se his taile reche sale	*Into; shall reach*
	all folk of France to mekill bale.	*woe*
	Thus have I mater for to make	*matter*
	for a nobill prince sake.	
	Help me, God, my wit es thin;	
20	now Laurence Minot will bigin.	
	A bore es broght on bankes bare	
	with ful batail bifor his brest;	*army*
	for John of France will he noght spare	
	in Normondy to tak his rest	
25	with princes that er proper and prest.	*fit and ready*
	Alweldand God of mightes maste,	*All-ruling; most*
	He be his beld, for He mai best,	*help*
	Fader and Sun and Haly Gaste.	
	Haly Gaste, Thou gif him grace,	*give*
30	that he in gude time may bigin	
	and send to him both might and space	
	his heritage wele for to win.	

51

And sone assoyl him of his sin,   *soon absolve*
hende God that heried hell,   *noble; harrowed*
35   for France now es he entred in,
and thare he dightes him for to dwell.   *prepares*

He dwelled thare, the suth to tell,
opon the coste of Normondy;
at Hogges fand he famen fell   *many fierce enemies*
40   that war all ful of felony.
To him thai makked grete maistri
and proved to ger the bare abyde;   *attempted to cause the boar to stop*
thurgh might of God and mild Mari,
the bare abated all thaire pride.   *lowered*

45   Mekill pride was thare in prese,   *throng of battle*
both on pencell and on plate,   *pennons; armor*
when the bare rade with outen rese   *haste*
unto Cane the graythest gate.   *Caen; most direct way*
Thare fand he folk bifor the gate,   [f. 55a[1]
50   thretty thowsand stif on stede.   *strong in that place*
Sir John of France come al to late;
the bare has gert thaire sides blede.   *boar has made their*

He gert blede if thai war bolde,
for thare was slayne and wounded sore
55   thretty thowsand, trewly tolde;
of pitaile was thare mekill more.   *infantry*
Knightes war thare wele two score
that war new dubbed to that dance.
Helm and hevyd thai have forlore;   *head; lost*
60   than misliked John of France.   *then was displeased*

More misliking was thare then,
for fals treson alway thai wroght;
bot fro thai met with Inglis men,
all thaire bargan dere thai boght.
65   Inglismen with site tham soght   *grief*
and hastily quit tham thaire hire,   *swiftly answered their investment*
and at the last, forgat thai noght,
the toun of Cane thai sett on fire.

Poem VII

That fire ful many folk gan fere, *fear*
70   when thai se brandes o ferrum flye; *see flames from afar fly up*
this have thai wonen of the were, *won; war*
the fals folk of Normundy.
I sai yow lely how thai lye, *faithfully*
dongen doun all in a daunce; *dashed*
75   thaire frendes may ful faire forthi *therefore*
pleyn tham untill John of France. *complain to*

Franche men put tham to pine *trouble*
at Cressy when thai brak the brig. *bridge*
That saw Edward with both his ine; *eyes*
80   than likid him no langer to lig. *remain*
Ilk Inglis man on others rig *Each; back*
over that water er thai went;
to batail er thai baldly big *bravely strong*
with brade ax and with bowes bent.

85   With bent bowes thai war ful bolde
for to fell of the Frankisch men.
Thai gert tham lig with cares colde; *made them collapse*
ful sari was sir Philip then.
He saw the toun o ferrum bren, *from afar burning*
90   and folk for ferd war fast fleand. *fear; fleeing*
The teres he lete ful rathly ren *quickly run*
out of his eghen, I understand. *eyes*

Than come Philip ful redy dight *prepared*
toward the toun with all his rowt; *troops*
95   with him come mani a kumly knight, *noble*
and all umset the bare obout. *beset*
The bare made tham ful law to lout *low; bow* [f. 55a[2]
and delt tham knokkes to thaire mede; *blows; reward*
he gert tham stumbill that war stout — *made them stumble*
100   thare helpid nowther staf ne stede.

Stedes strong bilevid still *remained*
biside Cressy opon the grene.
Sir Philip wanted all his will; *lacked entirely his desire*

53

	that was wele on his sembland sene.	*deportment*
105	With spere and schelde and helmis schene,	*glittering*
	the bare than durst thai noght habide;	
	the king of Beme was cant and kene,	*bold*
	bot thare he left both play and pride.	*merriment*

	Pride in prese ne prais I noght	*a crowd*
110	omang thir princes prowd in pall;	*robe*
	princes suld be wele bithoght	
	when kinges suld tham till counsail call.	
	If he be rightwis king, thai sall	
	maintene him both night and day	
115	or els to lat his frendschip fall	*allow*
	on faire manere and fare oway.	

	Oway es all thi wele, I wis,	*success, indeed*
	Franche man with all thi fare;	*airs*
	of murnig may thou never mys,	*sorrow; lack*
120	for thou ert cumberd all in care.	*burdened*
	With speche ne moght thou never spare	
	to speke of Ingliss men despite;	*scorn*
	now have thai made thi biging bare —	*dwelling*
	of all thi catell ertou quite.	*property; deprived*

125	Quite ertou, that wele we knaw,	*Compensated are you*
	of catell and of drewris dere;	*property; treasures*
	tharfore lies thi hert ful law,	*low*
	that are was blith als brid on brere.	*before; happy as a bird in a bush*
	Inglis men sall yit to yere	*this year*
130	knok thi palet or thou pas	*head*
	and mak the polled like a frere,	*you tonsured*
	and yit es Ingland als it was.	

	Was thou noght, Franceis, with thi wapin	
	bitwixen Cressy and Abuyle	
135	whare thi felaws lien and gapin	*gape*
	for all thaire treget and thaire gile?	*magic; guile*
	Bisschoppes war thare in that while	*time*
	that songen all withouten stole.	

	Philip the Valas was a file;	*coward*
140	he fled and durst noght tak his dole.	*portion*
	Men delid thare ful mani a dint	*dealt; blow*
	omang the gentill Genevayse;	
	ful many man thaire lives tint	*lost*
	for luf of Philip the Valays.	
145	Unkind he was and uncurtayse —	[f. 55b¹
	I prais no thing his purviance:	*management*
	the best of France and of Artayse	
	war al to dongyn in that daunce.	*destroyed*
	That daunce with treson was bygun	
150	to trais the bare with sum fals gyn.	*betray; device*
	The Franche men said all es wun!	
	Now es it tyme that we bigin,	
	for here es welth inogh to win	
	to make us riche for evermore,	
155	bot thurgh thaire armure thik and thin	
	slaine thai war and wounded sore.	
	Sore than sighed sir Philip;	
	now wist he never what hym was best,	*knew*
	for he es cast doun with a trip.	*false step*
160	In John of France es all his trest,	*faith*
	for he was his frend faithfulest;	
	in him was full his affiance,	*trust*
	bot sir Edward wald never rest	
	or thai war feld, the best of France.	*deposed*
165	Of France was mekill wo, I wis,	*truly*
	and in Paris tha high palays;	
	now had the bare with mekill blis	
	bigged him bifor Calais.	*lodged*
	Heres now how the romance sais	
170	how sir Edward oure king with croune	
	held his sege bi nightes and dais	*siege*
	with his men bifor Calays toune.	

[VIII]   **How Edward als the romance sais**
         held his sege bifor Calais.

	Calays men, now mai ye care,	*worry*
	and murnig mun ye have to mede;	*mourning shall; as reward*
	mirth on mold get ye no mare:	*earth*
	sir Edward sall ken yow yowre crede.	*teach*
5	Whilum war ye wight in wede	*Once; valiant; armour*
	to robbing rathly for to ren.	*at; quickly; run*
	Mend yow sone of yowre misdede;	
	yowre care es cumen, will ye it ken.	

	Kend it es how ye war kene	*Well known; bold*
10	al Inglis men with dole to dere.	*grief to injure*
	Thaire gudes toke ye al bidene;	*together*
	no man born wald ye forbere.	*spare*
	Ye spared noght with swerd ne spere	
	to stik tham and thaire gudes to stele.	*kill them*
15	With wapin and with ded of were	
	thus have ye wonnen werldes wele.	

	Weleful men war ye, I wis,	*Prosperous; truly*
	bot fer on fold sall ye noght fare.	*further; land*
	A bare sal now abate yowre blis	*boar* [f. 55b²
20	and wirk yow bale on bankes bare.	*woe; hills barren*
	He sall yow hunt als hund dose hare,	*hound*
	that in no hole sall ye yow hide;	
	for all yowre speche will he noght spare	
	bot bigges him right by yowre side.	*holds*

25	Biside yow here the bare bigins	
	to big his boure in winter tyde,	*build; bower; time*
	and all bi tyme takes he his ines	*dwelling*
	with semly sergantes him biside.	*soldiers*
	The word of him walkes ful wide —	*His renown spreads far and wide*
30	Jhesu save him fro mischance!	
	In bataill dar he wele habide	
	sir Philip and sir John of France.	

The Franche men er fers and fell *cruel*
and mase grete dray when thai er dight; *create great tumult; are prepared*
35 of tham men herd slike tales tell. *such*
With Edward think thai for to fight
him for to hald out of his right
and do him treson with thaire tales.
That was thaire purpos day and night,
40 bi counsail of the cardinales.

Cardinales with hattes rede
war fro Calays wele thre myle;
thai toke thaire counsail in that stede *place*
how thai might sir Edward bigile.
45 Thai lended thare bot litill while, *remained; time*
till Franche men to grante thaire grace.
Sir Philip was funden a file; *coward*
he fled and faght noght in that place.

In that place the bare was blith,
50 for all was funden that he had soght. *found*
Philip the Valas fled ful swith *quickly*
with the batail that he had broght. *army*
For to have Calays had he thoght
all at his ledeing loud or still, *command under any circumstances*
55 bot all thaire wiles war for noght —
Edward wan it at his will.

Lystens now and ye may lere, *learn*
als men the suth may understand, *truth*
the knightes that in Calais were
60 come to sir Edward sare wepeand —
In kirtell one and swerd in hand —
and cried sir Edward, thine are. *mercy*
Do now, lord, bi law of land
thi will with us for evermare.

65 The nobill burgase and the best *wealthy citizens*
come unto him to have thaire hire; *reward*
the comun puple war ful prest *ready* [f. 56a[1]

57

rapes to bring obout thaire swire.   *ropes; necks*
Thai said all, sir Philip oure syre
70   and his sun sir John of France
has left us ligand in the mire
and broght us till this doleful dance.

Oure horses, that war faire and fat,
er etin up ilkone bidene;   *everyone together*
75   have we nowther conig ne cat   *rabbit*
that thai ne er etin and hundes kene.   *fearless dogs*
All er etin up ful clene;
es nowther levid biche ne whelp —   *left bitch nor pup*
that es wele on oure sembland sene —   *is clearly seen in our appearance*
80   and thai er fled that suld us help.

A knight that was of grete renowne,
sir John de Viene was his name,
he was wardaine of the toune
and had done Ingland mekill schame.   *great*
85   For all thaire boste thai er to blame,
ful stalworthly thare have thai strevyn;   *stoutly; fought*
a bare es cumen to mak tham tame:
kayes of the toun to him er gifen.   *keys; given*

The kaies er yolden him of the gate;   *are yielded to*
90   lat him now kepe tham if he kun.
To Calais cum thai all to late,
sir Philip and sir John his sun.
Al war ful ferd that thare ware fun;   *terrified; found*
thaire leders may thai barely ban.   *curse*
95   All on this wise was Calais won;
God save tham that it so gat wan!

Poem IX

[IX] **Sir David had of his men grete loss**
with sir Edward at the Nevil cross.

Sir David the Bruse · was at distance
when Edward the Baliolfe · rade with his lance;
the north end of Ingland · teched him to daunce
when he was met on the more · with mekill mischance.   *moor*
5 Sir Philip the Valayse · may him noght avance;
the flowres that faire war · er fallen in Fraunce.
  The floures er now fallen · that fers war and fell;   *cruel*
  a bare with his bataille · has done tham to dwell.   *boar; army*

Sir David the Bruse · said he suld fonde   *attempt* [f. 56a²
10 to ride thurgh all Ingland, · wald he noght wonde.   *turn back*
At the West Minster hall · suld his stedes stonde,
whils oure king Edward · war out of the londe.
  Bot now has sir David · missed of his merkes   *desired ends*
  and Philip the Valays · with all thaire grete clerkes.

15 Sir Philip the Valais, · suth for to say,   *truth*
sent unto sir David · and faire gan him pray
at ride thurgh Ingland · thaire fo men to flay   *enemies to defeat*
and said none es at home · to let hym the way.   *hinder*
  None letes him the way · to wende whore he will,   *turn where*
20 bot with schipherd staves · fand he his fill.   *shepherds' staves*

Fro Philip the Valais · was sir David sent
all Ingland to win · fro Twede unto Trent.
He broght mani berebag · with bow redy bent;   *bag bearers*
thai robbed and thai reved · and held that thai hent.   *plundered; kept; seized*
25 It was in the waniand · that thai furth went;   *waning [of the moon]*
for covaitise of cataile · tho schrewes war schent.   *goods; scoundrels; confounded*
  Schent war tho schrewes · and ailed unsele   *pained unhappily*
  for at the Nevil cros · nedes bud tham knele.   *obliged; kneel*

At the Ersbisschop of York · now will I bigyn,
30 for he may with his right hand · assoyl us of syn.   *absolve*
Both Dorem and Carlele · thai wald never blin   *Durham; Carlisle; cease*
the wirschip of Ingland · with wappen to win.   *weapons*

59

Mekill wirschip thai wan, · and wele have thai waken,   *joy; awakened* [f. 56b[1]

for syr David the Bruse · was in that tyme taken.

35   When sir David the Bruse · satt on his stede,

he said of all Ingland · haved he no drede,

bot hinde John of Coupland, · a wight man in wede,   *noble; stout; armour*

talked to David · and kend him his crede.   *taught*

Thare was sir David · so dughty in his dede

40   the faire toure of Londen · haved he to mede.   *as reward*

Sone than was sir David · broght unto the toure

and William the Dowglas · with men of honowre;

full swith redy servis · fand thai thare a schowre,   *abundance*

for first thai drank of the swete · and sethin of the sowre.   *then*

45   Than sir David the Bruse · makes his mone —   *lament*

the faire coroun of Scotland · haves he forgone.   *crown*

He luked furth into France; · help had he none

of sir Philip the Valais · ne yit of sir John.

The pride of sir David · bigon fast to slaken,

50   for he wakkind the were · that held him self waken;   *war; allowed him no rest*

for Philyp the Valaise · had he brede baken,

and in the toure of Londen · his ines er taken.   *lodgings*

To be both in a place · thaire forward thai nomen,   *promise; pledged*

bot Philip fayled thare, · and David es cumen.

55   Sir David the Bruse · on this manere

said unto sir Philip · al thir sawes thus sere: *sayings diverse*

"Philip the Valais, thou made me be here;

this es noght the forward · we made are to yere.   *before this year* [f. 56b[2]

Fals es thi forward, · and evyll mot thou fare,   *agreement*

60   for thou and sir John thi son · haves kast me in care."

The Scottes with thaire falshede · thus went thai obout

for to win Ingland · whils Edward was out.

For Cuthbert of Dorem · haved thai no dout;

tharfore at Nevel cros · law gan thai lout.   *low; bow*

65   Thare louted thai law · and leved allane;

thus was David the Bruse · into the toure tane.   *taken*

Poem X

<table>
<tr><td>[X]</td><td>**How king Edward & his menye**</td><td>host</td></tr>
<tr><td></td><td>**met with the Spaniardes in the see**</td><td></td></tr>
</table>

I wald noght spare for to speke, · wist I to spede,	*hope to succeed*
of wight men with wapin · and worthly in wede	*brave; admirable in armour*
that now er driven to dale · and ded all thaire dede.	*grave; dead [despite]; deed*
Thai sail in the see gronde · fissches to fede.	*sea bottom*
5 Fele fissches thai fede · for all thaire grete fare;	*many; vaunting*
it was in the waniand · that thai come thare. [1]	

Thai sailed furth in the Swin · in a somers tyde,	
with trompes and taburns · and mekill other pride.	*trumpets and drums*
The word of tho werkmen · walked full wide;	
10 the gudes that thai robbed · in holl gan thai it hide.	*hiding place*
In holl than thai hided · grete welthes, als I wene,	
of gold and of silver, · of skarlet and grene.	

When thai sailed westward, · tho wight men in were,	*valorous*
thaire hurdis, thaire ankers · hanged thai on here. [2]	
15 Wight men of the west · neghed tham nerr	*approached nearer* [f. 57a[1]
and gert tham snaper in the snare — · might thai no ferr.	*made them stumble*
Fer might thai noght flit, · bot thare most thai fine,	*flee; die*
and that thai bifore reved · than most thai tyne.	*what; plundered; lose*

Boy with thi blac berd, · I rede that thou blin,	*advise; cease*
20 and sone set the to schrive · with sorow of thi syn.	*confusion*
If thou were on Ingland · noght saltou win;	
cum thou more on that coste, · thi bale sall bigin.	*coast; grief*
Thare kindels thi care; · kene men sall the kepe	*bold*
and do the dye on a day · and domp in the depe.	*cause you to; be dumped*

25 Ye broght out of Bretayne · yowre custom with care;	
ye met with the marchandes · and made tham ful bare.	*merchants*
It es gude reson and right · that ye evill misfare,	
when ye wald in Ingland · lere of a new lare.	*teaching*
New lare sall ye lere, · sir Edward to lout,	*obey (revere)*
30 for when ye stode in yowre strenkith · ye war allto stout.	*strength*

---

[1] *waning [of the moon] (an unhappy hour)*

[2] *their bulwark [to protect a crew in battle], their anchors, they hung on high*

61

[XI]   **How gentill sir Edward with his grete engines
wan with his wight men the castell of Gynes.**

War this winter oway, · wele wald I wene
that somer suld schew him · in schawes ful schene.   *thickets*
Both the lely and the lipard · suld geder on a grene.   *lily; leopard; gather*
Mari, have minde of thi man, · thou whote wham I mene.   *know*
5   Lady, think what I mene — · I mak the my mone —   *complaint*
thou wreke gude king Edward · on wikked syr John.   *avenge*

Of Gynes ful gladly · now will I bigin.
We wote wele that woning · was wikked for to win.   *know; dwelling* [f. 57a²
Crist, that swelt on the Rode · for sake of mans syn,   *died; Cross*
10   hald tham in gude hele · that now er tharein.   *health*
Inglis men er tharein, · the kastell to kepe,
and John of France es so wroth, · for wo will he wepe.

Gentill John of Doncaster · did a ful balde dede,   *daring*
when he come toward Gines · to ken tham thaire crede.   *teach*
15   He stirt unto the castell · with owten any stede;   *set out*
of folk that he fand thare · haved he no drede.
Dred in hert had he none · of all he fand thare;
faine war thai to fle · for all thaire grete fare.

A letherin ledderr · and a lang line,   *leather ladder*
20   a small bote was tharby · that put tham fro pine.   *boat; suffering*
The folk that thai fand thare · was faine for to fyne;   *eager to come to terms*
sone thaire diner was dight, · and thare wald thai dine.
Thare was thaire purpose · to dine and to dwell,
for treson of the Franche men · that fals war and fell.   *treacherous*

25   Say now sir John of France, · how saltou fare   *shall you*
that both Calays and Gynes · has kindeld thi care?
If thou be man of mekil might, · lepe up on thi mare,   *great*
take thi gate unto Gines · and grete tham wele thare.   *your way*
Thare gretes thi gestes · and wendes with wo;   *guests; go*
30   king Edward has wonen · the kastell tham fro.

Poem XI

Ye men of Saint Omers, · trus ye this tide   *pack up*
and puttes out yowre paviliownes · with yowre mekill pride.   [f. 57b[1]
Sendes efter sir John of Fraunce · to stand by yowre syde;
a bore es boun yow to biker · that wele dar habyde. [1]
      35   Wele dar he habide, · bataile to bede,   *offer*
          and of yowre sir John of Fraunce · haves he no drede.

God save sir Edward his right · in ever ilka nede,   *every*
and he that will noght so, · evil mot he spede!
And len oure sir Edward · his life wele to lede,   *grant*
      40   that he may at his ending · have hevin till his mede.   *reward*

A - M - E - N

---

[1] *A boar [King Edward] is prepared to fight you*

Notes

AMA = *Alliterative Morte Arthure*; SGGK = *Sir Gawain and the Green Knight*; SMA = *Stanzaic Morte Arthure*; YP = *The York Plays*. MS = Cotton Galba E.ix. Manuscript abbreviations have been silently expanded. All other editorial emendation, except punctuation and capitalization, is cited in the notes. For full references to Collette, Hall, Ritson, Scholle, James and Simons, Stedman, and Wright see the Select Bibliography.

[I]   **Lithes and I sall tell yow tyll**
       the bataile of Halidon Hyll.

Battle of Halidon Hill, 19 July 1333: Although often inaccurate in its details, Froissart's *Chronicle*, composed under the aegis of royal patronage, provides thumbnail sketches of events contemporary with Minot's poems. Froissart suggests some of the complex political background anteceding the Battle of Halidon Hill:

> There had been a truce between England and Scotland now for four years, the like to which had not occurred before for two hundred years: but the town of Berwick-upon-Tweed was destined to disturb it. David, who succeeded Robert Bruce on the throne of Scotland, held possession of Berwick, which Edward claimed as part of his own kingdom. The King of Scotland, who followed the advice of his council and chief barons on the subject, resolved that as King Robert, his father, had taken the town in open war from the late King Edward of England, and having kept possession of it during his lifetime, so he would do everything in his power to retain it; and such being the case, neither party was willing to give way. The contest which ensued, however, was fraught with dire misfortune to the Scots, for Edward advanced into their kingdom, destroyed it, and, having taken possession of Berwick, and also many other forts, placed in them several able and expert knights and squires, to protect the border countries. (p. 18)

Froissart glosses over the part played by Edward Balliol (son of King John Balliol, r. 1292–96) and "the Disinherited" in this renewal of hostilities. Led by Balliol and Henry Beaumont, a group of powerful Northern magnates (many of whom had lost holdings in the Lowlands by the 1328 Treaty of Northampton) defeated the Scots at Dupplin Moor in 1332. The Scots in turn having driven Balliol (crowned September, 1332) from the Scottish throne in favor of the young David II, Edward III allowed Balliol to muster support among the English. Hoping to draw Balliol from the siege of Berwick, established on 12 March 1333, the Scots invaded England on March 23, under the leadership of the new regent, Archibald Douglas, and threatened Bamburgh. Edward III arrived before Berwick after Easter, and on 19 July 1333, at the Battle of Halidon Hill, the Scottish army raised to relieve the siege was decisively defeated. Berwick surrendered, David II fled to France, and Balliol swore fealty to England. The Battle of Halidon Hill utilized Edward's strategy, to be employed again successfully on many occasions in the war with France, of waging battle from a defensive position with rows of archers and dismounted men-at-arms.

[1]   Rubrication is indicated by bold face text. Heading: Hall suggests *all* or *of* be inserted before *the bataile* in place of *tyll*.

4   *bute*. Hall notes that *bote* (adopted by Scholle) is the only form in rhyme, i.e., 4.58, 6.26.

5   *made midelerd and the mone*. See "made God medilerth and man," YP 9.158, and the lyric "Heghe Loverd, thou here my bone" from MS. Harley 2253, "that madest middelert ant mone," line 2.

6   *bestes and fowles*. Scholle emends to the alliterative formula *bestes and briddes*.

7   *socore*. Scholle, *socor*.

9   *droupe and dare*. An alliterative collocation found only in the rhyming romances and poems of the Alliterative Revival. See "bot ever droupe and dare," *AMA* line 4007, and "y droupe, y dare," *Tolous*, line 553.

10   *dern*. Hall suggests *derve*. Scholle reads *deds* for *dedes*, then *dose* for *done*.

12   *when Edward founded first to were*. Edward III (b. 1312, r. 1327–77; married Philippa of Hainault, a niece of Philip VI of France, in 1328). Edward agreed to support Balliol, and moved his administration to York, calling out the levies of four shires for the defense of the border and invading Scotland in the spring of 1333.

15   *sides sare*. See "on sides seere," YP 10.340, and frequently elsewhere.

17   *prise*. Scholle, Stedman, *pris*.

18   *boste*. Scholle, Stedman, *bost*.   *Normondye*. Scholle, *Normandye*.

19   *Thai sent thaire schippes on ilka side*. Minot seems to suggest here that the French promised to raise the siege of Berwick but fled before a single blow was offered. Thus is announced a major theme in Minot's poems, that the French are essentially cowards, their boasts empty words, their deeds but few. In fact, Philip VI of France had sent a fleet of ten ships to raise the siege, but it was destroyed by the English at Dundee, mentioned again in 2.24. From 1334 on, there were frequent threats of French retaliation; in August and September of 1335 rumors were rife that Philip VI had assembled a great fleet to attack the south coast of England.

21   *es noght at hide*. A rhyme tag typical of the rhyming romances.

22   *forto* is always one word in the MS.

24   *wurth*. Scholle, Stedman, *worth*.

25   *For*. MS: *ffor*; all initial double *f*'s are treated as majuscules.

30   *thareobout*. Scholle, *tharobout*.

33   *Jhesu*. MS: *ihu*. Scholle, *Iesu*; so too in 5.16. The scribe writes *ihesus* in full at f. 64a^2.

39   *dareand all for drede*. Scholle, *darand*. An alliterative collocation found elsewhere only in the rhyming romances and poems of the Alliterative Revival. Compare "dares for drede," *SGGK* line 315.

41   *Gai*. Scholle, *Gay*.   *thoght*. Collette, *thought*.

42   *on the Erle Morré and other ma*. Following the defeat at Halidon Hill, the nine-year old king, David II, and his mother fled to France. By 1335, the Earl of Moray, John Randolph, was regent for David II, and defeated an English expeditionary force under the Count of Namur on the hilltop in Edinburgh. The

Earl was later taken prisoner before Bamborough Castle and imprisoned in London.

45   *Philip Valays wordes wroght.* Through his mother, Edward was the grandson of Philip IV of France and the nephew of the last Capetian king, Charles IV, who died without an heir. Salic law, however, prohibited descent through the female line, and the French crown passed to Charles IV's cousin, Philip VI (r. 1328–50). In 1331, Edward had declared himself willing to perform liege homage to Philip VI for the duchy of Gascony, but in 1334 Philip VI insisted that discussion of the Scottish succession be included in any further Anglo-French negotiations. Edward responded by reasserting his title to the French crown; in 1340 he formally assumed the title "King of England and France." On the collocation *wordes wroght*, see "wroght neuere in worde," YP 13.181.

46   *suld.* Stedman, *said.*

49   *manasinges.* Scholle, *manasings.*

54   Oakden compares *stout on stede* with the phrase "stiff on stede," *SMA* lines 45, 350, and elsewhere.

56   *noght fer fro Berwik opon Twede.* City on the north-east coast at the mouth of the river Tweed.

60   *of wild Scottes and alls of tame.* Scholle, *wilde.* Hall suggests that Minot here makes a distinction between the Highland Scots, who spoke Gaelic, and the Lowland Scots, who spoke English.

62   *boste.* Scholle, Stedman, James and Simons, *bost.*

66   *at Dondé now es done thaire daunce.* Dundee, a city on the Firth of Tay in eastern Scotland. As Hall points out, *daunce* is one of Minot's repeated ironic tags (see for instance 5.14, 7.58, 7.74, 7.148–49, 8.72, and 9.3). Compare *Pearl*, lines 345–46: "For thogh thou daunce as any do, / Braundysch and bray thy brathez breme . . . ." For the collocation *done thaire daunce*, see YP 11.225; 19.96: "that daunce is done."

68   *France.* Hall notes that the nasalized *a* in Romance words before *mb*, *ng*, *nc*, *nd*, and *nt* is written either *a* or *au* in the MS, so both *France* and *Fraunce,*

chance and *chaunce*.

71, 87   *thing*. Collette notes that the scribe's normal practice is to use þ to represent *th*, but in *thing* he infrequently uses *th*.

75   *caitefes*. Stedman, *caitefs*. The alliterative collocation *cursed caitefes* occurs in fifteenth-century religious lyrics and in "cursid caytiffis," YP 30.356; 40.27; 47.317.

76, 81   *suth*. Scholle, *soth*.

77–78   *Sir Jon the Comyn had thai hid; / in haly kirk thai did him quell*. John Comyn was defeated by Robert Bruce in 1306 and subsequently murdered, 10 February 1306, in the Gray Friars' Kirk at Dumfries.

80   *dole er dight*. The phrase occurs in fourteenth-century lyrics and in "that doole schulde be dight," YP 26.184.   *that*. Hall suggests *thar*.

82   *menye*. Ritson, Wright, *menzé*. The word is dissyllabic and in 4.10 rhymes with *fre*.

87   *gaudes might no thing gain*. See "gaudis sall noght tham gayne," YP 11.248.

90   *proud in prese*. Scholle, Stedman, *pres*. An alliterative collocation found elsewhere only in the poems of the Alliterative Revival and the rhyming romances. See "prowde in prees," *Octavian the Emperor*, line 1641 and compare *prowd in pall* 7.110.

92   *pese*. Scholle, Stedman, *pes*.

[II]   **Now for to tell yow will I turn**
of the batayl of Banocburn.

MS omits *the*. Ritson's emendation.   *The Scottish victory at Bannockburn, 23–24 June 1314*: Minot's subject here is less the humiliating defeat of Edward II's English army by Robert Bruce and the Scots than it is the avenging of that defeat in the victory at Halidon Hill.

2   *at the Bannok burn*. Robbins gives the following verses, recorded in the *Brut*, with which Scots women taunted the English:

>   Maydenes of Engelande, sare may ye morne,
>   For tynt ye haue lost youre lemmans at Bannokesborn
>   (p. 262)

The English victory at Halidon Hill, in which large numbers of Scots but only a handful of English were killed, is celebrated by Minot as appropriate vengeance for the earlier defeat and the "Shameful Peace" of 1328.

3   *ye*. Ritson, *ze*. Throughout his edition, Ritson employs *z* for *ȝ*.

6   *yit*. Scholle, *yow*.

7   *Whare er ye, Skottes of Saint Johnes toune*. The Scottish city of Perth is so named because it contains a church dedicated to the saint.

8   *boste*. Scholle, Stedman, *bost*.

11   *worth*. Collette notes that the scribe usually uses the Southern form *wurth*.

13   *Skottes of Striflin*. The town of Sterling, near which was fought the Battle of Bannockburn. The castle of Sterling, held by the English, had been under siege since 1313. If not relieved by 24 June 1314, it was to be surrendered to the Scots.

15   *Now have thai, the pelers, priked obout*. Hall and Sisam suggest this line refers to Scots border incursions intended to distract Edward from the siege of Berwick.

17   *wurth*. Scholle, *worth*.

18   *bot ever*. Hall suggests *and ever*.

19   *Rughfute*. Scholle, *Rughfote*.

20   *berebag*. A derisive term for a Scot. Froissart explains:

The Scots are a bold, hardy race, and much inured to war. When they invaded England, they were all usually on horseback, except the camp followers; they brought no carriages, neither did they encumber themselves with any provision. Under the flap of his saddle each man had a broad plate of metal; and behind his saddle a little bag of oatmeal, so that when occasion needed, cakes were made of the oatmeal, and baked upon the plates; for the most part, however, they ate the half-soddened flesh of the cattle they captured, and drank water. (p. 13)

boste. Scholle, *bost*.

22   *Busk the unto Brig*. "Brig" is variously emended by editors, but it clearly represents the Flemish city of Bruges, capital of West Flanders in northwestern Belgium, not that the fleeing Scots hid under a bridge. But *n.b.* spelling in line 25. Ritson, Wright, and Scholle read *brig*. Hall, Stedman, James and Simon emend to *Brug*, and Collette to *Bruges*.

24   *Dondé*. Dundee, port in eastern Scotland in Angus on the Firth of Tay.

25   *The Skotte gase in Burghes and betes the stretes*. Minot's stark image of the defeated Scotsman in exile. Alone of the great cloth-making states in the Low Countries, Flanders owed allegiance to France rather than to the Holy Roman Emperor, and was ruled by the unpopular French count, Louis of Nevers. While the official position was pro-French and so favorable to the Scots, Flanders experienced great popular unrest. Louis of Nevers was driven into exile, replaced by a burgher, Jacob Van Artevelde, from whom Henry Burghersh, Bishop of Lincoln, obtained a promise of neutrality in 1337.

Skotte. MS. *skottes*.   *Burghes*. Ritson, Wright, Scholle, *burghes*.

26   *all thise*. Hall compares 3.47 and suggests *In all thise*.

harmes he hetes. See "Slike harmes hym for to hete," YP 18.136.

27   *men that he metes*. See "And many men myldely hym mette," YP 30.340.

28   *frendes he findes*. Compare "fynde me youre frende," YP 19.165, and "To fynde hym with oure frendis," YP 20.48.

29   *fune*. Scholle, *fone*.   *wurth*. Scholle, *worth*.

34   Scholle supplies *sir* before *Edward*.

[III]   **How Edward the king come in Braband**
        and toke homage of all the land.

        The sacking of Southampton, 4 October 1338: Between 1337 and 1339, the French raided at will Dover, Folkestone, Harwich, Hastings, Portsmouth, Rye, and the Isle of Wight, disrupting, among other things, wine importation. French ships were also reported in the mouth of the Thames; an order to drive piles into the river bottom as a precaution against invasion was issued in October, 1338.

2   *Ingland*. Scholle, *Ingeland*.

4   *grante*. Scholle, *graunte*.

11   MS: *trely*.

12   *into Brabant*. Scholle, *Braband*. Delayed three months for lack of shipping, Edward departed Walton-on-the-Naze for Antwerp on 16 July 1338. The allies acquired in the previous year by the embassy of Bishop Burghersh refused to act, however, until the emperor formally appointed Edward his suzerain in Germany and France.

13   *The kayser Lowis of Bavere*. Louis the Bavarian (1287–1347) elected Holy Roman Emperor as Louis IV in 1314. On 5 September 1338, at Coblenz, Louis IV invested Edward as his imperial vicar-general, a position with considerable authority over Germany and the Low Countries. Louis IV was paid £60,000 but did little to further Edward's cause. From 1341 on, he was allied with Philip VI.

15   *sons*. Scholle, *sunes*; Hall suggests emending to *He and his two sons also*.

17   *prelates*. Scholle, *prelats*.

19   *princes and pople*. The embassy of the Bishop of Lincoln and the Earls of Salisbury and Huntingdon won Edward the support of the Counts of Hainault, Gelderland, Berg, Cleves, and Marck, the Count Palatine of the Rhine, the Margrave of Juliers, and the Elector of Brandenburg, among others.

19   *ald.* Scholle, *old.*   *yong.* Scholle, *yung.*

21   *honowre.* Scholle, *honowr.*

25   Hall, Stedman, and James and Simons do not observe a new stanza here or at lines 49, 59, 85, 94, or 101, although the majuscules beginning these lines (except 101) are clearly decorated with the yellow ink wash which elsewhere indicates stanza divisions.

> *The duke of Braband.* John III, Duke of Brabant and Limburg (d. 1355) also promised support for Edward, at the cost of £60,000 and the promise to establish the wool staple at Antwerp. Froissart sums up:

> > On the feast of St. Martin King Edward had an interview with the Duke of Brabant at Arques. The town-hall was hung with rich and fine cloths. His majesty was seated five feet higher than the rest of the company, and had on his head a rich crown of gold. Here letters from the emperor to the king were publicly read, by which the King of England was constituted and established vicar of the empire of Germany, with full power granted him to do all acts of law and justice to every one in the emperor's name, and also to coin gold and silver. All persons, moreover, were commanded to do him fealty and homage as vicar of the empire. (p. 20)

31   *al.* Stedman, *all.*

36   *thare ogayne.* Scholle, *tharogayne.*

37   *his moné that was gude and lele.* Froissart alludes to the cost of bribery in winning the support of Jacob Von Artevelde in the Low Countries:

> > By fair speeches, promises, and a bountiful distribution of money, Edward, through his agents, at last prevailed with this powerful individual so far, that by his means the chiefs of the principal towns gave their consent that the King of England and his army might pass through Flanders whenever he pleased. . . . (p. 19)

> The authority to coin money granted by Louis IV allowed Edward to establish a mint at Antwerp which produced golden *écus* bearing the eagle of the Empire over Edward's own name.

40   *better.* Scholle, Stedman, *bet.*

42   *I wis.* Hall, *i-wis.*

46   *whilk*. Ritson, *whilke*.

47   *bithoght*. Wright, *bithought*.

49   *sone*. Scholle, *son*.

56   *childe*. Scholle, Stedman, *child*.

59   *At Hamton*. Southampton and Portsmouth were raided in 1337–38; Froissart gives the details:

> A party of French troops, consisting of Sir Hugh Quiriel and some few others, made a somewhat similar attack [*i.e.*, to that of Sir Walter Manny's earlier attack on the French town of Mortaigne] upon England. As soon as they heard that hostilities had commenced, they landed one Sunday morning in the harbour of Southampton, entered the town whilst the inhabitants were at church, pillaged it, and having loaded their vessel with booty, fell down with the tide, and made sail to Dieppe, where they went on shore, and divided the plunder. (p. 21)

60   *gaylayes*. Hall notes this as a mistake for *galayes*.

62   *mekill*. Wright, *makill*.

67   *stareand*. Scholle, *starand*.

68   *knoked*. Stedman, James and Simons, *knokked*.

69   *with tham*. Hall suggests emending to "something like *tham likes now nan other gle, (Cursor, 54).*" *none*. Wright, *non*.

70   *might*. Stedman suggests *moght* as more likely.

        fain . . . fle. See "I am ferde be my feyth and fayne wolde I flee," YP 28.265.

71   *suth*. Scholle, *soth*.

75–76   *whare Cristofer stode / at Armouth*. The contemporary chronicler Adam of Meerimuth reports that the great cog *Christopher* (300 tons, 3 cannon) was taken by the French on the Tuesday before the sack of Southampton, although other reports have it taken off Middleburg with the *Edward* and two smaller bullion ships, the *St. George* and the *Black Cock,* as they were returning home from the sale of the year's wool crop. Yarmouth is on the Isle of Wight.

76   *Armouth*. Scholle, *Aremouth*.

77   *went*. MS: *wen*. Hall, following Wright, emends to *went*.

78, 97   *galayes men*. Scholle, *galaymen*.

80   *and with tham als war tarettes two*. Scholle, *tarets*. The taret, like the galley, was a large ship propelled by rowers (the Genoese galleys under the command of Boccenera [see 10.19 note] were particularly fast and deadly in combat) but was primarily a transport vessel. Galiots were small galleys, and cogs like the *Cristopher* and *Edward* were beamy, deep-draft ships of the line.

84   *mens*. Scholle, Stedman *mennes*.

86   *sone*. Scholle, *son*.

91   *schippes*. Scholle, *schips*.

   ful. Hall notes this should be omitted, a suggestion followed by Stedman, James and Simons.

93   *wane*. Scholle, *wone*, and in the next line, *one*.

96   *baldly*. Scholle, Stedman, *baldely*.

99   Collette supplies *So* at the beginning of the line.

100   *with owten*. The scribe's word divisions are often inconsistent.

107   *nane*. Scholle, *none,* and in the next line *mone*.

112   *whils*. Ritson, *while*; Wright, *whil*.

114   *untill*. Stedman, *until*.

116   *gude*. Scholle, *gode*.

118 *lifes.* Stedman, *lives.*

122 *gude.* Scholle, *gode.*

125 MS: *ihc. Ingland.* Scholle, *Ingeland.*

126 *haly hand.* Wright, *holy.* The phrase occurs in fifteenth-century religious lyrics and in "with his holy hand," YP 17.43.

[IV] **Edward oure cumly king**
    in Braband has his woning

    Edward's first invasion of France; the Battle of Flamengerie, 23 October 1339: On 1 September 1339, Edward sent a ceremonious challenge to Philip, whose army was at Compiègne. With his allies, Edward marched through Valenciennes towards Cambrai, the first of a number of long raids or *chevauchées* in which the English laid waste the countryside.

1 Note in MS opposite this line: *Ewd III p. 103*, a reference to Warton.

2 *Braband.* The Braband, what is now central Belgium, was a wealthy province caught between English and French loyalties. The region was of strategic importance to the English wool industry. It was battle ground for the disastrous Norwich Crusade later in the century.

3 *cumly.* Hall notes this is probably a mistaken repetition from the first line.

5 *ordanis.* Scholle, *ordaynes*; Ritson, Wright, *ordains.*

8 *grant.* Scholle, *graunt. gaste.* Scholle, *gast.*

9 *his heritage to win.* At Ghent in January 1340, Edward formally assumed the title to the Crown of France; his "heritage" is another of Minot's formulas for the dual monarchy. Wright prints the following Epigram on the Assumption of the Arms of France:

    Jus E. regis Angliae in regno Francorum
    Rex sum regnorum bina ratione duorum;

Anglorum cerno me regem jure paterno;
Jure matris quidem rex Francorum vocor idem.
Hinc est armorum variatio bina meorum,
M. ter centeno cum ter denoque noveno.
  (*Pol. Poems,* I, 26.)

[The Right of Edward King of England in the Realm of France.
I am king of the two realms for a twofold reason.
I regard myself a King of England by right deriving from my father.
I am indeed styled King of France by right on my mother's side.
Hence come my two coats of arms in the year 1340. (James and Simons, p. 85)]

12   Ritson omits the first *and.*

16   *langer wil.* Stedman, *longer will.*

17   *fast will he fare.* Compare "forthe faste to fare," YP 5.173.

18   *grapes.* The Brabant is not known for its vineyards, but served rather as the mustering point for Edward's attack on France. England was a great importer of wines in the fourteenth century, especially from Burgundy and Gascony. The French king's disruption of the trade in the 1330's had nearly doubled the price in the latter part of the decade, with only about a third of the quantity in 1333–34 (6166 tons) being imported in 1339–40 (2022 tons). With the truce in September 1340, prices dropped to a pre-war level and wine was plentiful again in England. See Margery Kirkbride James, *Studies in the Medieval Wine Trade* (Oxford: Clarendon Press, 1971), pp. 19–34.

19   *ferd.* Scholle, *fered;* Hall suggests that *ferd* is "practically dissyllabic."

20   *God.* Scholle, *Iesus.*

22   *nobill.* Scholle, *nobil.* Scholle inserts *als* after *duc.*

25   *floure de lice.* Scholle, *flour de lis. de lice* is one word in MS. The *fleur de lys* was the heraldic symbol of the French kings. See *A European Armorial,* ed. Rosemary Pinckes and Anthony Wood (London: Heraldry Today, 1971), pp. 68, 88.

26   *wan.* Scholle, *gained.*

27   *fast he fled for ferde.* See 7.90, *ferd war fast fleand,* and compare "for ferdnes may we flee," YP 47.122.

28   *right.* Scholle, *righte.* Hall suggests emending to *rightwis,* see 7.113.

       aire. Scholle, *hair.*

32   *wit.* Scholle, *with.*   *in.* Hall, comparing *Wyntoun's Chronicle,* v. 3153, suggests *into.*

33   *batale.* Scholle, *bataille.*

34   *his men.* Perhaps repeated from line 32. Scholle emends to *He bad tham tham purvay*; Hall suggests *He bad his menye tham purvay.*

35   *lenger.* Scholle, *leng.*

37–38   *He broght folk ful grete wone, / ay sevyn oganis one.* MS: *boght.* Advancing toward Peronne, Philip occupied Edward's county of Ponthieu with a massive army. What Minot characterizes as Philip's cowardice may have been politic caution, for Edward's allies, notoriously unreliable, probably posed no long-term threat.

38   *oganis.* Ritson, Wright, *ogains*; Scholle, *ogaynes.*

39   *wapnid.* Ritson, Wright, *wapind.*

40   MS: *whe.* Ritson, *when.*

42   *than durst he noght cum nere.* On 23 October 1339, near the village of Buironfosse, Edward deployed his forces in the formation that had proved so successful at the Battle of Halidon Hill: knights dismounted and banks of archers enfilade. Froissart reports that Philip was discouraged from the attack by an unfavorable forecast which arrived from his uncle, the renowned astrologer King Robert of Sicily. Perhaps Philip also suspected an English trap. In any event, Philip forbore the attack.

43   *mornig.* Hall notes this may be a genuine form and so James and Simons.

44   *Ingliss.* MS: *igliss.*

45   *changed*. MS: *shanged*.

47   *gude*. Scholle, *god*.

50   *stalwortly*. Ritson, *stalworthly*.   *schelde*. Scholle, *scheld*.

54   *frek to fight*. A collocation found only in the rhyming romances; compare
          "frekke for to fighte," *The Siege of Milan,* line 1430.

55   *sir*. Written above the line in MS.

56   *walld*. Scholle, Stedman, *wald*.

57   *gayned*. Hall suggests *gamed*.

61–62   *It semid he was ferd for strokes / when he did fell his grete okes*. In the first
          English military dispatch to survive, Edward writes angrily to his son, the Black
          Prince: "Whereupon the foe withdrew his van and gave orders to encamp, made
          trenches around him and cut down large trees in order to prevent us approach-
          ing him" (Packe, p. 86). Philip had previously replied to Edward's challenge that
          if Edward "would choose out a place not fortified with trees, ditches or bogs,
          the King of France without fail would afford him battle." This failure to live up
          to the terms of the challenge is seized upon by Minot as further evidence of
          Philip's perfidy.

63   *pavilyoune*. Scholle, *pavilyoun*.

66   *doune*. Scholle, *doun*.

67   *The king of Beme had cares colde*. Philip's great army included three kings: blind
          King John of Bohemia, Philip's cousin Philip of Evreux, King of Navarre (line
          70), and the young exile David of Scotland.

68   *ful*. MS: *fur*; James and Simons supply a second *ful* before *bolde*.

69   Scholle inserts *for* after *stede*.

70   Ritson, Stedman, and Collette supply *He and* at the beginning of the line.

71   *war faire feld in the ferene*. The line is probably corrupt. Skeat suggests that *feld* may mean struck down (followed by Collette and James and Simons) or is perhaps an error for *fled*. Hall thinks that *Faire* is a scribal error for *fain* and *for*, and proposes to read *"War fain for fered in the ferene."* Scholle emends *feld* to *felid*, and Stedman proposes *"War faire fayn in the ferene."* Hall suggests the words *feld in the* were inserted later, but examination of the MS under ultraviolet light reveals no sign of scraping. For another example of a king hiding in fear in the heather, see the note to 9.34.

74   *felde hat*. Scholle, *felde it hat.*   *Flemangrye*. Scholle, *Flamengerye*.

77   *dukes that war doghty*. See "my duke doughty," YP 30.30.

79   *raw*. Scholle, *row*, and in the next line, *blow*.

89   *hied him hame*. Compare "Hamward I rede we hye," YP 20.9, and "hye you hame," YP 16.191.

90   *giff*. Stedman, *gif*.

91   *the lely flowre*. That is, Philip, King of France.

92   *halely*. Scholle, *hally*.

93   *sogat*. Ritson, *so gat*; Stedman, James and Simons, *so-gat*.

95   Collette omits *that*.

96   *berde*. Scholle, Stedman, *berd*.

[V]   **Lithes and the batail I sal bigyn**
       of Inglisch men & Normandes in the Swyn

The Battle of Sluys, 24 June 1340: On Saturday 24 June 1340, a fleet of two hundred and sixty English ships attacked the French flotilla anchored at Sluys (now Vissingen) in the mouth of the river Zwin. Once ships had engaged, medieval naval battles were simply land-battles fought across decks, and the ships of the French fleet were chained together by squadrons, a tactic that provided more room for maneuvering troops. It also meant that an entire line of ships could be taken at once, as were the French at Sluys. The chronicle of Geoffrey Le Baker de Swynebroke provides the details:

> An iron cloud of bolts from crossbows, and arrows from bows, fell upon the enemy, bringing death to thousands; then those who wished, or were daring enough, came to blows at close quarters with spears, pikes and swords; stones, thrown from the ships' castles, also killed many. In brief, this was without a doubt an important and terrible naval battle which a coward would not have dared to see even from afar off. The sheer size and height of the Spanish ships rendered useless many of the blows cast by the English; but, finally, the first French squadron was defeated, abandoned by its men, and then captured by the English. The French ships were all chained together, so that they could not be separated from one another; thus only a few English ships were needed to guard one group of those which had been abandoned, the remainder being better able to direct their attention to the second French squadron, attacking it with some difficulty. None the less, this squadron was to be disabled even more easily than was the first, for the French abandoned their ships, large numbers of men jumping, of their own accord, into the sea. The first and second squadrons thus overcome, and with the light giving way to dusk, the English, since it was getting dark and they were very exhausted, decided to leave matters as they were until the morrow. (Allmand, pp. 128–29)

The Battle of Sluys was a notable English victory; the French flagship, *Saint-Denis*, was taken, and the *Christopher* recaptured along with the *Edward*. In all, two hundred and thirty ships fell into English hands. Shortly thereafter, Edward commemorated this victory with the minting of the first English gold coin, the noble, whose obverse shows Edward, armed with sword and shield, standing in his cog, *Thomas*; on the shield are quartered the arms of England and France.

1   *Minot with mowth.* Minot here refers to himself by name for the first time. It should be noted that the alliterative phrases *mene with mouthe*, as well as *mele with mouthe* and *munne with mouthe*, are important survivals from early Middle English alliterative poetry in the poems of the Alliterative Revival. Their use here links Minot's poems to a long practice of alliterative composition. Like the phrase "as I in toun herde, / with tonge" from *SGGK*, lines 31–32, however, these phrases should not be taken as self-evident testimony for an oral poetic tradition.

2   *suth sawes and sad.* Compare "the soth sawe," YP 33.288.

          mens. Scholle, *mennes.*

4   *sorow suld slake*. The phrase occurs in fourteenth- and fifteenth-century religious lyrics and in "do my sorowe to slake," YP 39.45.

6   *bute*. Scholle, *bote*.

7   *Valas*. Scholle, *valays*.

8   *sir Hugh Kyret*. Hugh Quièret, appointed Admiral of France in 1336. He died of his wounds at the Battle of Sluys.

13   *ferd*. Scholle, *fered*.

14   *thare lered Inglis men tham a new daunce*. One of Minot's favorite ironic tags. See note to 1.66.

     MS: *anew*. The scribe not infrequently runs *a* into a following *n*; see *aname*, line 16. Collette omits *tham*.

15   *buriase*. Ritson and Wright, *burjase*; Scholle, *burias*.

17   *Sluse*. Scholle, *Sluys*.

18   *Normandes*. Scholle, *Normands*.

19   *Bruges*. Stedman, James and Simons, *Brug*.   *Ipyre*. Scholle, *Ipres*.   *hereof*. Scholle, *herof*.

20   *Edward . . . that was in Arwell*. King Edward had returned to England in February of 1340 and called upon Parliament to raise further monies, troops, and ships for the war effort. Edward was prepared to sail again for Antwerp from Orwell at Whitsun, but word came of the great French fleet assembled at Sluys. Edward commandeered sixty additional ships and finally sailed on 22 June 1340.

22   *sergantes*. Scholle, *seriantes*.

23   *Normandes*. MS: *Nomandes*. Scholle, *Normands*; Stedman, *Normandes*.   *war*. Stedman, James and Simons, *were*.

25   *sune.* Stedman, *sone.*

26   *barons.* Scholle, *barouns.*

27   *Thai come byfor Blankebergh on Saint Jons night.* On 23 June, off Blankenburgh, the English first caught sight of the French fleet. Aboard his flagship the *Thomas*, King Edward saw "so great a number of ships that their masts seemed to be like a great wood." Battle commenced on 24 June, the feast of St. John the Baptist — half-ebb (5.33) occurred at roughly 3 p.m. and high tide was around 11:30.

28   *well.* Scholle, *wel.*   *sary sight.* Compare "I am sorie of a sight," YP 29.41.

30   *the wilde waniand.* The period of the waning moon was considered to be unlucky. See 9.25 and 10.6 for other instances of this use. In a note to "The Battle of Neville's Cross," line 25, Robbins cites the *Brut* on the Scots' defeat in 1422 at Vernon: "But the moste vengeance fell upon the proude Scottes. . . So that they may say wele 'In the croke of the mone went thei thidre warde, And in the wilde wanyende come thei homewarde'" (p. 265). See also the Wakefield Master's *The Second Shepherds' Play*: "Now walk in the wenyand!" line 405.

31   *suth.* Scholle, *soth.*

32   *meri.* Ritson, *mery.*   *sir Robard out of Morlay.* Robert de Morley, second Baron Morley (1296?–1360). Commanded in 1338 to guard Yarmouth from the French fleet, Robert was shortly thereafter made Admiral of the Fleet from the Thames to Berwick. As such, he commanded at the Battle of Sluys. He was also present at the Battle of Crécy.

34   *Normandes.* Scholle, *Normands.*

36   MS, Ritson, and Wright: *es.* Hall suggests the error is due to the subsequent *es.* Collette emends *wreches* to *wretches*, Scholle to *wrecches*; James and Simons emend the second *es* to *is.*

37   *The erle of Norhamton.* William de Bohun (1312?–1360). One of the seven earls belted in 1337, William was appointed one of the commissioners to treat with Philip of France on Edward's claim to the French crown; subsequently, he was

appointed a commissioner to treat with Robert Bruce. He took part in Edward's expedition of 1338 and in 1342 was appointed the king's lieutenant and captain-general in Brittany. He was present at Crécy. William died 16 September 1360, and was buried at Walden in Essex.

erle. Scholle, *Erl.*

38   *man.* James and Simons, *men.*

39   *Sir Walter the Mawnay.* Sir Walter de Manny, a native of Hainault, was knighted in 1331. He distinguished himself in the Scottish campaign, particularly at the siege of Berwick. On 11 August 1337 he was appointed Admiral of the Fleet north of the Thames, and according to Froissart, he was the epitome of valor and courage at the Battle of Sluys. He was created a baron of the realm in 1347 and Admiral of the Northern Fleet in 1348. The most distinguished soldier of his time, he died in 1372.

40   Scholle supplies *man* after *bold*; Hall suggests *burne*, Stedman *barn.*   *batayl.* Ritson, *batayle.*

41   *The duc of Lankaster.* Henry of Lancaster (1299–1361). Famed as a youthful crusader in Prussia, Rhodes, Cyprus, and Granada, Henry was appointed to command an army against the Scots in 1336. On 16 March 1337, Edward created him Earl of Derby, and he was present at Sluys where according to Froissart he behaved with great valor. In 1345 Derby was made lieutenant and captain of Aquitaine, and in the same year he succeeded his father as Earl of Lancaster and of Leicester and steward of England. (He was not titled Duke until 1352, evidence that Minot apparently revised the whole series, perhaps adding the rubrics, when he composed the final poem.) Lancaster was present at the siege of Calais and was one of the original knights of the Order of the Garter. He was accounted a perfect knight, the greatest warrior of his time. His daughter and heiress Blanche married John of Gaunt, and her death by plague is commemorated in Chaucer's *Book of the Duchess.* It has been suggested that Chaucer's portrait of the knight in the General Prologue of *The Canterbury Tales* is modeled on Henry of Lancaster.

41   Hall does not indicate a stanza here; Stedman and James and Simons do.

42   *mani.* Wright, *many.*

43   *stalworthly*. James and Simons, *stalworthy*. *stint*. Stedman suggests *stert*.

44   *Normandes*. Scholle, *Normands*; also 50, 61, and 68.

46   MS: *C*. Ritson, *hundred*; Scholle, *hundreth*.

47   *Sir Wiliam of Klinton*. William Clinton participated in Edward's first Scottish campaign and was created Earl of Huntingdon in 1337. In April of that year he accompanied Henry Burghersh, Bishop of Lincoln, as ambassador in the Low Countries. He was later made an Admiral, Justice of Chester, Governor of Dover, and Warden of the Cinque Ports. He died in 1354.

    Wiliam. James and Simons, *William*.

49   *it semid with thaire schoting als it war snaw*. The English longbow again proved its superiority. Froissart's account does not glorify the battle:

> The French were equally desirous to engage, and as soon as they were within sight of the English, they filled the *Christopher*, the large ship which they had captured but a short time before, with trumpets and other warlike instruments, ordering her to begin the attack. The battle was fierce, murderous, and horrible. In the end the English came off victorious, the *Christopher* was recaptured by them, and all in her taken or killed. (p. 25)

53   *The gude erle of Glowceter*. Hugh de Audley, b. 1289?, created Earl of Gloucester 1337. Audley was present with Edward at Buironfosse and accompanied Henry of Derby's expeditionary force to Bordeaux in August of 1345. Badly wounded at Poitiers, Audley died in 1347. Stedman, however, identifies the "gude erle" as James de Audley or Audeley (1316?–1369).

    mot. James and Simons, *mote*.

54   *boldmen*. Scholle, *bolde men*; Stedman, *bold men*.

55   *baldely*. Scholle, *boldely*.

56   James and Simons supply *the* before *middes*.

57   *wretches*. Wright, *wrecches*.

59 *John Badding*. Hall and particularly Stedman argue that Badding "was probably a personal friend of Laurence Minot." Roscoe E. Parker identifies Badding as John Badding of Winchelsea, officially a master of the galley from the Cinque Ports (*PMLA* 37 [1922], 360–65).

60 *suthwest*. Scholle, *southwest*.

63 *John of Aile*. Jan van Eyle, a citizen of Sluys, commander of the French forces aboard the *Christopher*. He was captured in the battle and subsequently beheaded.

64 *was comen into Cagent*. Scholle, *cumen*. Probably Cadzant, a village in Zeeland near the mouth of the Scheldt. Cadzant was earlier the site of a famous English attack on the garrison of the Count of Flanders in November of 1337, in which Sir Walter Manny rescued the fallen Earl of Derby. Compare *cantly and kene* with 7.107 and see YP 22.183, "cant and kene."

65 *Bot*. James and Simons, *bote*.

67 *swith*. Scholle *swithe* and in the next lines *skrithe*, *kithe*.

71 *on*. Ritson and Wright, *in*.

72 *had*. Scholle, *haved*.   *won*. Scholle, *wonnen*.

73–74 *The kogges of Ingland war broght out of bandes / and also the Cristofir*. In addition to the *Christopher*, the English recovered the *Edward*, the *St George*, the *Black Cock*, and the *Rich Oliver*.

74 *also*. Scholle, *als*.

75 *In*. A large decorated initial at the top of column b. Hall and James and Simons mark the stanza break two lines later where *Sir Edward* also has a large black initial decorated with yellow. Collette marks the stanza break at line 75.   *still*. Ritson, *stil*.

76 Stedman and Hall, *Til*. James and Simons supply *that* following *til*.

77 *wurthi*. Scholle, *worthli*.

78   *flude*. Scholle, *flode*.

     faire mot him fall. See "And felawes, faire mott ye fall," YP 29.214.

80   *gudely*. Scholle, *godely*, also in following line.

81   *God gif*. Compare "God giffe you myght and mayne," YP 10.135.

82   *oure*. Ritson, *our*. *gude*. Scholle, *gode*.

84   *whare*. Ritson, Wright, Scholle, *where*. *Normandes*. *r* is interlinear in the same hand. *made*. Scholle, *maked*.

85   *Wele*. Wright, *wale*.

86   *boste*. Stedman, James and Simons, *bost* and in 87.

88   *sawls*. James and Simons, *sawles*. *sais*. Wright, *said*.

[VI]   **Herkins how king Edward lay
with his men bifor Tournay.**

The Siege of Tournai, July to September, 1340: Toward the end of July, 1340, Edward and his allies invested Tournai, which had been impressively fortified and garrisoned. Froissart provides a summary of the siege:

> At the time appointed the King of England set out from Ghent, accompanied by seven earls from his own country, two prelates, twenty-eight bannerets, 200 knights, 4,000 men-at-arms, and 9,000 archers, without counting foot soldiers; these with the fine cavalry of the Earl of Hainault and the 40,000 Flemings of Jacob Von Artaveld, completely invested the city of Tournay. The siege lasted a long time, and many gallant actions were performed. . . . (p. 26)

Heading: *Herkins*. MS: *herknis* (?); Collette, *Herkin*.

1   *Towrenay*. Scholle, James and Simons, *Towrnay*.

3   *bore*. Only here and in 7.21, but *bare* sixteen times. *brenis*. Ritson, Wright, *brems*.

A bore with brenis bright. Collette suggests that the reference to the boar is based on the Prophecies of Merlin in Geoffrey of Monmouth's *Historia Regum Britanniae*, which foretells the conquest of Gaul by an English boar. In the English poem which derives from Merlin's prophecies in Geoffrey, *The Prophecy of the Six Kings to follow King John*, Edward III is identified as both lion and boar. See notes to 7.1. Minot's reference to Merlin seems not to be idiosyncratic but rather part of a larger pattern of political propaganda. Geoffrey Le Baker, for instance, works in an offhand allusion to the prophecy in his description of the attack at Sluys: ". . . he [Edward III] began to attack the enemy as they had hoped he would. A fearful shout arose into the sky above the wooden horses [the French ships], as Merlin had prophecied" (Allmand, p. 128).

5   *semely.* Scholle, *semly.*

6   *schilterouns.* In 5.63 *scheltron* and so Scholle. Hall notes that the scribe has followed the analogy of Romance words like *resoun, soun.*

7   *domes day es dight.* Compare "dome this day is dight," YP 47.186.

15   *harmes.* Scholle, *harms.* Hall suggests rather that *harmes* is dissyllabic here as in 2.26, and omits *that.*

16   *hele.* Hall suggests *holde*, and in 17, *holdes.* But more likely *hele* is simply the indicative form of *helen*, "to cover or conceal."

19   *find ye yowre frende.* See "fynde me youre frende," YP 19.165.

21   *sall* occurs sixteen times; *sal* only at 5.6, 6.33 and 8.19.

23   *now thar.* Scholle, *No bowes er for yow bende.*

27   *mirthes mun ye mis.* The phrase occurs in fifteenth-century secular lyrics and in the York plays: compare "my mirth may noghte mys," YP 1.83.

30   *and.* Scholl, *all.*

31   *I wis.* Hall, *i-wis.*

33   *sal.* James and Simons, *sall.*

34   *dintes*. Scholle, *dints*.   *dowte*. Collette, *dowt*.

35–36   *Yowre biginges sall men brene / and breke yowre walles obout*. Scholle, *bigings*; James and Simons, *bigines*. Scholle, *bren*. Although the outlying country was plundered and largely destroyed, Tournai itself was successful in resisting the siege, which lasted, Froissart says, three days short of eleven weeks, a truce finally having been arranged on 25 September 1340 by Philip's sister, Lady Jeanne de Valois. These lines seem to suggest that Minot composed the poem before the siege was withdrawn.

39   *care men sall yow ken*. Compare "slyk care was neuere kende," YP 11.260.

40   *lord to lout*. Compare "lord for to lowte," YP 33.8.

41   *yowre*. MS: *yow*.

44   *als*. James and Simons, *as*.

45   *fande*. Scholle, Stedman, *fand*.

48   *broght on bere*. Compare "For be thou, blissid birde, unto bere broght," YP 44.50.

50   *than cumes Philip to late*. Scholle, *then*. Having marched from Arras, Philip and his army encamped at Bouvines, some ten miles to the west of Tournai, but declined once again to offer battle.

52   *hert ye may him hate*. Compare "Hartely we hym hate," YP 26.97.

54   *till*. Scholle, *til*.   *Turnay*. Scholle, *Tournay*.

56   The MS has a mark of punctuation between *strate* and *ful* and also after *still*.

60   *trow my tale*. Compare "Are schalle I trowe no tales," YP 41.163.

61   *tuke*. Scholle, *toke*.

62   MS: *brwed*. Scholle, Stedman, James and Simons *brewd*; Collette, *brewed*.

A Braban. John, third Duke of Brabant, a powerful but duplicitous ally of Edward. He seems to have allowed many civilians from Tournai to pass through his lines to join the French at Arras; there were also rumors that he permitted supplies to enter the city. His treachery may have been one of Edward's reasons for abandoning the siege.

64   *Giftes grete*. Compare "gifte is not grete," YP 16.343.

67   *rapely ride*. Scholle, *raply*. See "full rappely I ridde," YP 16.7.

70   *moste for mede*. Scholle, *most*. Compare "mater moste were for oure mede," YP 20.68.

71   *frely fode*. This collocation occurs in fourteenth-century religious lyrics as well as in the York plays, "And I myght fynde that frely foode," YP 15.78, and "that frely foode," YP 19.110.

74   *thare in*. Scholle, *tharin*; Hall, *tharein*.

77   *main and mode*. Wright, *maine*. An alliterative phrase found also in Old English poetry and prose, the poetry of Layamon, and the rhyming romances.

78   *France*. Scholle, *Fraunce*.

80   *grante*. Scholle, *graunte*.

[VII]   **How Edward at Hogges unto land wan
and rade thurgh France or ever he blan**.

Saint Vaast-la-Hougue, 11 July 1346; Caen, 30 July 1346; Battle of Crécy, 26 August 1346: Edward brought to Normandy a large army, perhaps exceeding 15,000 men, many of whom were Welsh and Cheshire archers. The army had been mustered in the expectation of reinforcing Henry of Lancaster in Aquitaine and raising the siege of Aiguillon. According to Froissart, Edward was persuaded to land in Normandy by Godfrey de Harcourt, who promised little resistance and easy plunder.

Headnote: MS: *tlurgh*.

1–2   *Men may rede in romance right / of a grete clerk that Merlin hight*. Stedman, *romaunce*. The creation of Geoffrey of Monmouth (*Historia Regum Britanniae*, *Vita Merlini*), Merlin as magician and prophet acquires preeminence in a number of twelfth- and thirteenth-century romances, notably Robert de Boron's *Merlin*, the anonymous *Suite du Merlin*, and the English *Arthour and Merlin*. Geoffrey introduced into the *Historia* a list of Merlin's prophecies from which derives in its various Latin, Anglo-Norman, and English stages *The Prophecy of the Six Kings to follow King John* recorded on folio 49a of Cotton Galba E.ix, only two leaves before Minot's poems. Taylor notes that *The Six Kings* was the prophecy used against Henry IV by the Percy-Glendower faction (*The Political Prophecy in England*, p. 48).

2   *grete*. Scholle, *gret*.

3   *wreten*. Scholle, *writen* and in next line *witen*.

5   Hall observes that *yit* seems to mark these two lines as an interpolation of the scribe.

6   *men*. James and Simons, *man*.

8–9   *Out of the north into the sowth / suld cum a bare over the se*. The Six Kings characterizes Edward III as a Lion fierce and terrible of heart and as the Boar of Prosperity, Nobility, and Wisdom, who will whet his tusks on the gates of Paris.

11   *the se*. Wright, *these*.

13   *France*. Scholle, *Fraunce*, and so in lines 16, 23, 35, *etc*.

14   *wrath*. Scholle, *wroth*.   *tharein*. Scholle, *tharin*.

15   *Untill*. Scholle, *until*.

17   *mater for to make*. Compare "This matere makes me," YP 16.246.

18   *prince*. Scholle, *princes*. Hall notes the *s* is dropped because another *s* follows.

20   *now Laurence Minot will bigin*. See the Introduction for the Minots of Yorkshire

and Norfolk.

23   *for John of France will he noght spare*. John of France (b. 1319, r. 1350–64), Duke of Normandy.

24   *Normondy*. Scholle, *Normandy,* and so in 38, 72, *etc.*

26   *maste*. Scholle, *mast.*

27   *mai*. Wright, *may.*

28   *Gaste*. Scholle, *gast*, and so in 29.

30   *gude*. Scholle, *god*. Beginning at this line, the scribe marks stanzas by marginal notation.

33   *assoyl*. James and Simons, *asoyl.*

35   *entred*. Wright, *entrid.*

37   *suth*. Scholle, *soth.*

39   *at Hogges fand he famen fell*. As early as New Year's Day, 1346, Edward gave orders for the fleet to assemble at Portsmouth, but not until July 11, after a week of bad weather had kept them at sea, did the English land at the little sea-port on the coast of Normandy, Saint-Vaast. The surprised town offered no resistance and soon the whole Cotentin peninsula was overrun, and unwalled towns like Barfleur and Cherbourg sacked and pillaged.

40   *ful*. James and Simons, *full.*

41   *makked grete maistri*. Scholle, *maked* and *gret*. Compare "he makis on this molde mekill maystrie," YP 31.108, and in many other places.

43   *mild Mari*. A commonplace of the lyrics and the York plays; see "of mylde Marie," YP 25.522, and many other instances.

45   *prese*. Scholle, Stedman, *pres.*

46   *pencell*. Scholle, *pencel*.

47   *with outen*. James and Simons, *withouten*.   *rese*. Scholle, Stedman, *res*.

48   *unto Cane the graythest gate*. By the end of July, Edward had taken the unwalled city of Caen.

51   *Sir John of France come al to late*. Duke John with a large army had gone south in February 1346 to attack the cities of Aquitaine held by Henry, Earl of Lancaster and his garrisons, and laid siege to Aiguillon on April 5. Indeed, one of Edward's objectives in the invasion of Normandy was to draw John north, raising the siege at Aiguillon and rescuing Lancaster. Duke John however did not break off the siege until August 20, and he did not return to Paris until September.

53   Hall supplies *tham* after *gert*, following Morris and Skeat's *Specimens*; so too James and Simons.

55   *tolde*. Scholle, *told*.

56   *was*. James and Simons, *war*.

57   *war*. James and Simons, *was*.

58   *dance*. Scholle, *daunce*.

61   *misliking*. MS: *misliling*.

62   *treson*. Scholle, *tresoun*.

63   *Inglis men*. James and Simons, *Inglismen*.

64   *bargan dere thai boght*. Scholle, *der*. See "This bargan sall be bought," YP 9.126.

65   *Inglismen*. James and Simons, *Inglis men*.

70   *o ferrum*. Hall, *o-ferrum*; Collette, *oferrum*.

71   *wonen*. Scholle, *wonnen*.

72   *fals*. Scholle, *false*.

73   *how*. Wright, *now*.   *lye*. Scholle, *ly*.

74   *dongen doun*. Scholle, *dungen*. Compare "to be dong doune," YP 33.331.

75   *faire*. Scholle, *fair*.

78   *at Cressy when thai brak the brig*. Hall suggests that *Cressy* is a scribal error for Poissy. Philip and his army lay on the north of the Seine at Rouen, Edward on the south. The bridge at Poissy was the last before Paris, and on 13 August Philip crossed the bridge and had it demolished as he retreated to Paris. The piers were not destroyed, however, and the English were able to repair the span.

80   *than*. Stedman suggests the MS may read *then*, but close examination does not support such a reading. *langer*. Scholle, Stedman, *leng*, a reading Hall endorses but does not adopt.

83   *baldly*. Scholle, *boldly*.

85   *bent*. Scholle, *bended*.

87   *tham*. James and Simons, *them*.

90   *ferd war fast fleand*. See 4.27.

93   *Than*. Wright, *Then*.

94   *toward the toun*. Wright, *town*. The town is Paris.

95   *kumly knight*. See "comely knyght," YP 25.514.

104   *sembland sene*. James and Simons, *seen*. Compare 8.79 and see "no sembelant be sene," YP 16.149.

105   *schelde*. James and Simons, *scheld*.   *helmis*. Stedman, *helmes*.

106   James and Simons supply *thai* following *bare*.

107   *cant and kene.* See 5.64.

109   *prese.* Stedman, *pres.*

110   *prowd in pall.* A phrase found elsewhere only in the rhyming romances; see "proud yn palle," *Libeaus Disconus*, lines 389, 1835, and compare *proud in prese* 1.90.

111   *princes suld be wele bithoght.* Minot offers here a critique of those princes — William, Count of Namier, Henry, Count of Salm, and John of Hainault — whose allegiance shifted from Edward to Philip between 1340 and 1346.

112   *till counsail call.* See "ne counsaille to call," YP 29.300.

       kinges suld. Hall notes that *suld* "is clearly due to the preceding line, as ten Brink points out in Scholle, p. 45." *till.* MS: *toll.* Ritson, *tyll*; Hall, *till.* *counsail.* James and Simons, *counsaill.*

113   *sall.* Scholle, *sal.*

115   *els.* Scholle, *elles*; James and Simons omit the initial *or.*

117   *I wis.* Ritson, Hall, *i-wis* and so line 165.

119   *murnig.* Hall, *murni[n]g*; Collette, *murning*; Stedman, James and Simons, *murnig.* Compare "that other es chastynig of fless," MS f. 69b.

121   *speche . . . spare.* See 8.23 and 10.1 and compare "at my speche wolde thou never spare," YP 6.139.

124   *catell.* Scholle, *catel.*

127   *lies . . . ful law.* The phrase may be found in the Harley lyrics and in the York plays, "and laies hym full lowe," YP 16.6; or "lay thaim full lowe," YP 16.26.

131   *mak.* Collette, *make.*

133–34 *Was thou noght, Franceis, with thi wapin / bitwixen Cressy and Abuyle.* James and Simons, *nought.* By the 17th of August, the English had repaired the bridge at

Poissy, and the army moved north across the Seine, heading for the Somme and a rendezvous with Edward's Flemish allies. Philip marched from Saint-Denis two days later. Between Abbeville and Amiens, Edward could find no crossing of the Somme, but finally a French informant revealed a ford at Blanchetaque manageable at low tide. The French holding the north bank were defeated by Hugh Despenser and Northampton in the vanguard while high tide prevented Philip's pursuit. The French and English armies finally met in the valley of the Maye (known as the Vallée aux Clercs) on 26 August 1346. Edward again employed the tactics so successful in Scotland, positioning his forces on the high edge of the forest of Crécy-en-Ponthieu — the right flank under the command of the Black Prince, the left flank under the Earl of Northampton. The pursuing French army, almost entirely cavalry, attacked late in the afternoon, uphill and into the glare of the setting sun.

137 *Bisschoppes war thare.* Thomas de Hatfield, the Bishop of Durham, was one of the military commanders at Crécy.

140 *tak.* James and Simons, *take.*

141 *delid . . . dint.* The phrase may be found in poems of the Alliterative Revival and the rhyming romances. Compare "delen dyntes," *Laud Troy Book*, line 9233, and "dyntes to dale," *SMA*, line 1076.

142 *the gentill Genevayse. a* corrected out of *e* in the MS; Scholle, *Genevays.* Running out of ammunition, the Genoese crossbow mercenaries fell back, only to be trampled by the charging French knights.

146 *purviance.* James and Simons, *purviaunce.*

147 *the best of France and of Artayse.* Scholle, *Artays.* In the chaotic battle that followed, which continued until dark, the flower of French chivalry was cut down. The Count of Flanders, the blind King of Bohemia, the Count of Blois, Philip's brother, Duke of Alençon, Ralph, Duke of Lorraine, John, Earl of Harcourt, lay dead on the field. Altogether the English heralds identified 1,542 mounted knights killed. King Philip, twice dismounted, twice wounded, and twice rescued, escaped with his retinue to Amiens to rally the remainder of the army.

148 MS: *alto dongyn.* Scholle, *dungyn*; Hall, *al to-dongyn.*

151   *wun*. Scholle, *won*.

154   *evermore*. Scholle, *evermare* and in line 156, *sare*; but see 7.54, 57, 59.

155   *armure*. Collette, *armur*.

        thik and thin. The collocation occurs elsewhere only in the rhyming romance *Sir Degare*, line 188.

157   *Sore*. Scholle, *Sare*.

158   *hym*. Hall, *him*.

160   *es*. Scholle, *was*.

161   *frend faithfulest*. The collocation "faithful friend" occurs in fourteenth-century religious lyrics and frequently in the York plays: "frende faithtfull," YP 16.335, *etc*.

166   Ritson supplies *the* before *high palays*.

168   *bigged him bifor Calais*. With Duke John and his army nearing Paris, Edward, still without having met with his Flemish allies, moved north again to besiege Calais.

169   *romance*. Scholle, *romaunce*.

[VIII]   **How Edward als the romance sais
held his sege bifor Calais.**

The Siege of Calais, 1346–1347: For Minot, Calais is the home port of channel piracy and the origin of the French depredations along the English coast during the late 1330's and early 1340's. He presents the siege of Calais as just retribution for earlier acts of lawlessness. Froissart gives an account of the siege:

> Edward marched with his victorious army to Wisant, and having halted there one whole day, arrived on the following Thursday before the strong town of Calais, which

Notes

the King of England, he collected together all the poorer inhabitants and sent them out of the town in order that the provisions of the place might last the longer; he resolved moreover to defend the town to the last. (p. 49)

Unlike the unwalled cities on the Cotentin peninsula, Calais was strongly fortified, defended by a double curtain wall, a double dike, and a fully provisioned and garrisoned citadel. The town could not be taken by force; Edward resolved to reduce it by starvation, investing the city with a siege and naval blockade. The citizens surrendered on 4 August 1347 and the Truce of Calais was signed at the end of September.

Title: This poem is VII in Ritson, VIII in Scholle, Collette, James and Simons, and VIII or VIIb in Hall.

1   *Calays*. Ritson and Scholle, *Calais*.

2   *murnig*. Hall, *murni[n]g*; Collette, *murning*. See 7.119.

4   *sall*. Scholle, *sal*.

6   *ren*. James and Simons, *run*.

8   *care es cumen*. See "Oure cares ar comen," YP 6.46; 45.227; or "What care is comen," YP 15.39.

11   *gudes*. Scholle, *godes*; MS: *albidene*.

14   *gudes*. Scholle, *gods*.

17   *I wis*. Hall, *i-wis*.

19   *sal*. Stedman, *sall*. *abate yowre blis*. See "blisse schal neuere abatte," YP 19.71.

21   *hunt als hund dose hare*. See the complaint in MS Harley 2253, "The Song of the Husbandman," "honteth ase hound doth the hare," line 56, which is also an example of iteration or stanza-linking.

23   *speche . . . spare*. see 7.121 and 10.1. Compare "Such speking wille we spare," YP 20.203.

26 *to big his boure in winter tyde.* To shelter his troops through the winter months of the siege, Edward had constructed near the bridge of Nieulay a grand wooden encampment, Villeneuve-le-Hardi; Queen Philippa joined him there shortly before Christmas.

27 *takes he.* James and Simons, *he takes.*

28 MS: *segantes.* Ritson, Hall, *sergantes*; Scholle, *seriantes.*

29 *walkes ful wide.* Compare 10.9 and "walked full wyde," YP 30.299.

30 MS: *ihu.* Ritson, *Jhesu*; Wright and Scholle, *Iesu.* *fro.* Collette, *from.* *mischance.* Scholle, *mischaunce.*

31 *dar.* Ritson, *dare.*

32 *sir Philip and sir John of France.* Scholle, *Fraunce.* As early as April, 1347, Philip and John began to assemble a force to relieve Calais, including those who had survived Crécy as well as Duke John's southern army. On 27 July, Philip's troops arrived at Sangatte, separated from the English forces by the river Hem.

34 *grete.* Scholle, *gret.*

37 *hald.* Scholle, *hold.*

40 *bi counsail of the cardinales.* Pope Clement VI sent two cardinals, Annibale Ceccano, Bishop of Frascati, and Etienne Aubert, later Pope Innocent VI, to discuss a treaty between England and France.

41 *Cardinales.* Scholle, *Cardinals.*

44 *how thai might sir Edward bigile.* Minot here reflects English distrust of the papal court at Avignon.

45 *bot.* James and Simons, *bote.*

46 *grace.* Collette, *gr_ac_e.*

47 *Sir Philip was funden a file.* Scholle, *founden.* Negotiations for a treaty failed,

and Philip offered battle. On 2 August, however, a day before the armies were to meet, the French army melted away, chased by Lancaster and Northampton.

50   *funden*. Scholle, Stedman, *fun*; *that* is omitted by Wright.

51   *Valas*. Scholle, *Valays*.

54   *all*. James and Simons, *al*.   *ledeing*. Scholle, *leding*.

55   *all*. James and Simons, *al*.

57   Ritson continues this as VII, Scholle and Stedman as VIII; Hall calls it VIIc but continues it as VIII.

58   *suth*. Scholle, *soth*.

60   *sare wepeand*. Scholle, *sar wepand*.

61   *In kirtell one and swerd in hand*. Scholle, *on*. Robbins cites the *Brut* on the appearance of the emissaries:

> [they] wenten on the walles of the toun, and in other divers placys, as naked as they were bore, saf here chirtys and brechys, & heldyn hire swerdus naked, & the poynt downward, in hire handes, & puttyn ropys & halterys abowte hire neckys, and yolden up the keyes of the toun and of the Castell to Kyng Edward, with grete fere and drede of hert. (p. 267)

Froissart reports the famous story of the Burghers of Calais:

> Edward, at first, was unwilling to accept anything but an unconditional surrender of all the inhabitants to his will; at the remonstrance of Sir Walter Manny, however, he agreed to have placed at his absolute disposal six only of the principal citizens, who were to come out to him with their heads and feet bare, with ropes round their necks, and the keys of the town and castle in their hands; upon this being complied with, the rest were to receive his pardon. After some hesitation six citizens were found ready to purchase the freedom of their fellow-sufferers upon these hard terms. They left the town in the way appointed by the king, who received them with angry looks, and ordered their heads to be struck off without delay: all who were present entreated him to have mercy, but he replied that the Calesians had done him so much damage and put him to so much expense, that it was proper they should suffer for it; and without doubt these six citizens would have been beheaded had not the

queen, on her knees and with tears in her eyes, entreated him to spare them. (p. 50)

On 28 September 1347, a truce was signed outside the walls. Almost all the inhabitants of Calais were dispossessed; English colonists were offered easy and generous terms, and the city remained in English hands over the following two hundred years.

62   *and cried sir Edward, thine are.* Ritson, *thine we are*, and so Wright, Scholle, Hall and Stedman; Hall notes that the MS "is perhaps right." James and Simons, following Stedman and Hall, suggest *are* here derives from Old English *ar*, "mercy," citing *Octavian*: "The Crysten prysoners were full fayne, / When the Sarsyns were y-slayne, / And cryed, 'Lord, thyn ore!'" (lines 1681–83). The form *are* is preserved in the Northern dialect as late as 1400: "Lord Alexander, thine are, quare is thi wittis?" *The Wars of Alexander*, line 5361.

65   *nobill.* Ritson, *noble*; Scholle, *nobil.   burgase.* Scholle, *burias.*

67   *puple.* Scholle, *pople.*

69   *Thai said all.* Hall suggests *Than said thai all, Philip oure syre.*

70   *France.* Scholle, *Fraunce.*

72   *till.* James and Simons, *til.   dance.* Scholle, *daunce.*

73–74 *Oure horses, that war faire and fat, / er etin up ilkone bidene.* James and Simons, *were.* Despite the practice of expelling the "bouches inutiles" and the permeability of the English blockade, the citizens of Calais suffered greatly from lack of food. The formula repeated in the *Brut*, "they eten hors, houndes, cattes & mys" may originate with a message for Philip from John de Vienne [8.82] recovered in the wreckage of a French convoy destroyed off Calais by John Montgomery's ships. John de Vienne writes to King Philip, "Know, dread Sir, that your people in Calais have eaten their horses, dogs, and rats, and nothing remains for them to live upon, unless they eat one another. Wherefore, most honourable Sir, if we have not speedy succour, the town is lost" (Packe, p. 169).

76   *hundes.* Scholle, *houndes.*

78   *nowther.* Scholle, *nowþer.*

79   *sembland sene*. Compare 8.79 and "sembelant be sene," YP 16.149.

81   *renowne*. Scholle, *renown*.

82   *sir John de Viene*. Jean de Vienne, seigneur de Pagny (d. 1351). Warden of Calais and a veteran of French expeditions to Scotland, he fought with John of France in Normandy in 1341.

83   *wardaine*. Scholle, *wardain*.   *toune*. Scholle, *toun*.

85   *boste*. Stedman, *bost*.

86   *strevyn*. Scholle, *strivyn*.

87   *mak*. James and Simons, *make*.

88   *gifen*. Scholle, *given*.

94   *barely*. Scholle, *barly*.

96   MS: *so gat*, and so Ritson. Hall, Stedman, James and Simons, *so-gat*; Collette *sogat*.

[IX]   **Sir David had of his men grete loss**
        with sir Edward at the Nevil cross.

The Battle of Neville's Cross, 17 November 1346: The battle was fought about a kilometer west of Durham Cathedral. The English army formed its ranks on a ridge somewhat south of Crossgate Moor, southeast of Baxter Wood and within sight of Bearpark. The Scots were on lower ground to the northwest. A chronicler from Lanercost Abbey provides an account (colored no doubt by the Scots' sacking of his abbey):

> About the third hour, on a field hard by Durham, the English host came upon the Scots, led by the Earl of Angus in the front line, a man of noble stock and valiant, ever ready to do battle for his country. The Bishop ordered that no man should spare a Scot and he himself rode against them with such a staff [mace] that without confession he absolved many Scots of all future trouble in this world. Then amid the blare of trumpets, the clash of sword on shield, the hurtling of arrows, you might

hear the wailing of the wounded. Arms were broken, heads shattered, many lay dead upon the field. Before the hour of Vespers the battle was over and those Scots who had not fallen, fled. David, who called himself King of Scotland, was taken and sent in chains to the Tower. (Neillands, p. 107)

Collette (p. xxxiii) points out that Minot's poem is very close to a contemporary Latin poem on the same subject and that they share the metaphor of flowers that have fallen:

> *Si valeas paleas, Valoyes, dimitte timorem;*
> *In campis maneas, pareas, ostende vigorem.*
> *Flos es, flore cares, in campis viribus ares,*
> *Mane techel fares, lepus es, lynx, non leo pares.*
> *Francia flos florem, caput olim nobiliorum,*
> *Jam contra mores leopardus tollit honores.*
> *Subpedito florem, rapio florentis honorem,*
> *Flos fueram, formido feram cun jubare veram.*

[If you are worth anything, Valois, put aside fear. Stay in the field, be obedient, display your energy. You are the flower, you have lost the flower, your strength has dried up; *Mane, Techel, Phares.* You are a horse, a lynx: you do not look like a lion. France is the flower of flowers, the capital once of those of nobler birth. Now, against his nature, the leopard carries off the honours. I supply the flower, I seize the glory of him that prospers. Once I was the flower: now I fear the real beast with its splendour. James and Simons, p. 96]

Wright reproduces the MS lineation by half-line but numbers pairs of half-lines. I have followed Hall and Stedman in printing long lines, as in the other poems, with a dot marking the caesura.

1   *Sir David the Bruse.* David II, (b. 1324, r. 1329–71), son of Robert the Bruce. Following the defeat of the Scottish army at Halidon Hill (see poem 1), David II had gone with his mother to France for safe-keeping, where he remained until 1341. The phrase *at distance* may mean "far removed," a reference to David's French exile. On the other hand, the phrase may also mean "in opposition, hostile to," in which case the opening of this poem may refer to the battle at Dupplin Moor, in which Edward Balliol and "the Disinherited" defeated the Scots on 12 August 1332. Dupplin Moor may be *the more* referred to in line 4; otherwise *the more* refers to Crossgate Moor, west of Durham, where the Battle of Neville's Cross was fought.

to in line 4; otherwise *the more* refers to Crossgate Moor, west of Durham, where the Battle of Neville's Cross was fought.

distance. Scholle, *distaunce*, and *launce* in the next line.

2   *Edward the Baliolfe*. Scholle, *Baliolf*. Edward Balliol the pretender (see poem 1, notes).

3   *the north end of Ingland*. Edward had foreseen the possibility of renewed hostilities in the North as a result of his French expedition, and he had therefore refrained from mustering the levies in the counties north of the Trent.

4   *mischance*. Scholle, James and Simons, *mischaunce*.

5   *Sir Philip the Valayse · may him noght avance*. *Valayse*. Scholle, *Valys*. *avance*. Scholle, *avaunce*. Philip had supplied David with both men and money in the hope of creating a distraction in England. Even before Crécy, the Scots were raiding over the border, but in October, in response to summonses from Philip (one dated 20 June 1346 and a later one from Saint-Denis, dated 22 July), David mustered his army, seized Liddell, sacked Lanercost Abbey, and appeared before Durham (see line 16).

6   *flowres . . . faire*. Scholle, *fair*. An alliterative collocation frequent in secular and religious lyrics of the thirteenth and fifteenth centuries as well as in the York plays: compare "With flouris fayr," YP 2.71.

9   *suld*. Ritson, *sulde*.   *fonde*. Scholle, *fande*.

10   *to ride thurgh all Ingland*. Although a large English army (numbering perhaps 15,000) was assembled to meet the Scots, it was all that stood between the invading forces and the rest of England north of the Trent (see line 22).

   wonde. Scholle, *wande*.

11   MS: *west minster*. Hall, *Westminster*; Collette, *West Minster Hall*.   *stonde*. Scholle, *stande*.

12   Wright supplies *onde* as the initial word; Hall suggests "perhaps *Whils Edward oure king*."   *londe*. Scholle, *lande*.

15   *suth*. Scholle, *soth*.

17   MS: *fo men*. Scholle, *famen*; Hall, James and Simons, *fomen*. *flay*. Ritson, *slay*. Scholle supplies *all* before *Ingland* and so Stedman in brackets.

19   *whore*. Scholle, Stedman, *whare*.

20   *schipherd staves*. Ritson, Wright, *schiperd staves*; Collette, *Schipherd*.

22   *fro Twede unto Trent*. Collette, *from*. That is, the North Midlands of England. The river Tweed forms the border between England and Scotland; the Trent cuts across the midlands.

26   *for*. Collette, *fro*. *cataile*. Scholle, *catail*.

27   Hall does not begin a new stanza here.

28   *for at the Nevil cros*. The Battle of Neville's Cross was fought on or near Crossgate Moor, west of Durham Cathedral.

29   *At the Ersbisschop of York*. Defense of the northern borders had traditionally been the responsibility of the Archbishops of York. The incumbent, William Zouche (Edward's Keeper of the Privy Seal [1335] and Treasurer [1340]) was appointed to the see of York in 1340 by Pope Clement VI despite Edward's preference for William de Kildesby. He was a military commander of some distinction and fought gallantly at Neville's Cross.

31   *Both Dorem and Carlele*. A number of editors suggest that Minot here means not the bishops but the men of these towns, for Thomas de Hatfield, the Bishop of Durham, was in France and neither he nor John de Kirkby, the Bishop of Carlisle, is listed among the twelve English commanders commended by Edward. Minot is not alone, however, in placing the Bishops of Carlisle and Durham at the scene of the battle; Froissart puts Thomas de Hatfield in command of the first division with the Marcher lord Henry Percy of Northumberland, and the poem "Durham Field" includes both Bishops of Durham and Carlisle as commanders.

32   *wappen*. Scholle, *wapen*.

34   *syr David the Bruse · was in that tyme taken*. Cut off from his troops, wounded, and fleeing the field, David was captured by John Copeland, but not before he knocked out two of Copeland's teeth. A less heroic account of his capture is given in the Latin poem recounting the battle, printed by Wright:

Notes

Copland arestat David cito se manifestat.
  (*Pol. Poems*, I, 46).

[David the Bruce runs away; as he flees, the lion turns and roars. Copeland strikes David in flight and wraps him in wounds. Copeland hounds David, finds the king in the thorn bushes, and arrests him as soon as he shows himself.]

For the alliterative collocation *tyme taken*, see "tyme of the takyng," YP 29.216.

37   *hinde John of Coupland.* Scholle, Stedman, James and Simons, *hende.* John Copeland was a Northumberland squire, later sheriff of the county, and one of the commanders of the third English division. He was rewarded for his capture with an annuity of £500, made constable of Roxburgh Castle and elevated to a knight-banneret.

38   One line in the MS.

40   *the faire toure of Londen.* Scholle, *tour* and so in 41; *London.* Recovered of his wound, David was finally surrendered to Sir Thomas Rokeby, High Sheriff of Yorkshire, and brought to the Tower of London in late December, 1346.

41   *Sone.* Scholle, *Son.*

42   *William the Dowglas.* Sir William Douglas (d. 1353). A relative of the Earls of Douglas, Sir William was called "The Flower of Chivalry" and the "Knight of Liddesdale." A brilliant border campaigner for the Scots, he was commander, with the Earl of Murray, of the second division at Neville's Cross, where he was captured. Imprisoned in the Tower of London for seven years, he finally swore fealty to Edward.

     honowre. Scholle, *honour.*

43   *full.* James and Simons, *ful.*   *schowre.* Scholle, *schowr.*

44   *sethin.* MS: *seuin* or *senin*, the latter adopted by Ritson, Wright, and Scholle; all other editors emend to *sethin.*

46   *coroun.* Scholle, Stedman, *croun.*

47   *luked.* Scholle, *loked.*

48   *sir* omitted by James and Simons.

49   *bigon.* Scholle, *bigan*; Hall suggests *bigon fast for to slaken.*

51   *Valaise.* Scholle, *Valais.*   Hall inserts *his* before *brede.*

52   *toure.* Scholle, *tour.*   *ines.* Scholle, *innes.*

53   *nomen.* Scholle, Stedman, *numen*; Hall offers *thaire forward had thai numen.*

54   *fayled thare.* Scholle, *thare fayled.*   *cumen.* Wright, *cumin.*

57   One line in the MS; the half-line is marked by a *punctus elevatus.*

59   *Fals es thi forward.* Compare "false forward is feste," YP 27.101.

60   *son.* Scholle, *sun*; Hall suggests *thi son* seems superfluous.   *haves.* Scholle, *has.*

61   *Scottes.* Scholle, *Skottes.*

63   Cuthbert of Durham. Saint Cuthbert, monk and Bishop of Lindisfarne (c. 634–87). His remains were translated to a Saxon church at Durham in 999 and again in 1104 into the new Norman cathedral. The prior of Hexham, placing a holy cloth used by St. Cuthbert on a spear point, displayed it like a banner on the battle field, a relic to whose miraculous powers the victory was ascribed (Hall, pp. 91–92).

64   *tharfore.* Collette, *Tharefore*; Scholle inserts *the* before *Nevel.*

65   *Thare.* Hall, *Thaire.*

66   *toure.* Scholle, *tour.*

[X] **How king Edward & his menye
met with the Spaniardes in the see**

Les Espagnols-sur-mer, off Winchelsea, 30 August 1350: Froissart gives the details
of the encounter:

> About the time of the celebration of this marriage [Earl Lewis of Flanders, who had
> been betrothed to Edward's daughter, Isabella, fled to France and married a
> daughter of the Duke of Brabant], there was much ill will between the King of
> England and the Spaniards, on account of their repeated pillages at sea. It happened
> that a Spanish fleet had been to Flanders with merchandise, and was about
> returning, when Edward, who hated the Spaniards greatly on account of the injuries
> they had done to him, thus addressed his lords: "We have for a long time spared
> these people, but they do not amend their conduct; on the contrary, they grow more
> arrogant; for which reason they must be chastised as they repass our coasts." His
> lords readily assented to this proposal, and a fleet was prepared to meet the
> Spaniards on their return. The Spaniards had intelligence given them of the King of
> England's intention; however, they were quite indifferent about it, for they were very
> good sailors, and had well provided themselves with all sorts of warlike ammunition,
> such as bolts for crossbows, cannon, bars of forged iron, and large stones. When they
> weighed anchor, the wind was favourable, and it was a fine sight to see their forty
> vessels of such a size, and so beautifully under sail. The English fleet, which was well
> prepared under the command of the king himself and Lord Robert de Namur, met
> the Spaniards off Calais. The Spaniards had the wind in their favour, and might
> easily have declined the battle, if they had so preferred; but they disdained to sail by,
> and as soon as they saw the English, bore down upon them, and commenced the
> fight: well and bravely it was fought on both sides till nightfall — many were cut to
> pieces, and many drowned; however, victory declared for the English. The Spaniards
> lost fourteen ships, and the others saved themselves by flight. (pp. 53–54)

2   *wight.* Scholle, *wighte.*

3   *ded all thaire dede.* Compare "dye for alle our dede," YP 11.404.

4   *sail.* Collette, *sall.*   *see gronde.* Scholle, *seeground*; Hall, *see-gronde.*

6   *it was in the waniand · that thai come thare.* By some accounts, the Castilian
     fleet appeared off Winchelsea in the early evening, about the time of
     Vespers. See 5.30 for the reference to the waning of the moon.

7   *Thai sailed furth in the Swin · in a somers tyde.* Under the command of Charles de la Cerda, the Spanish fleet was returning to Spain from the mouth of the River Sluys in Zeeland laden with Flemish merchandise and the spoils of various attacks on English wine and wool shipping.

8   *trompes and taburns.* Scholle, *trumpes.* The collocation occurs frequently in poems of the Alliterative Revival and rhyming romances but not elsewhere. See "trumpetts and tabretts," *Scotish Feilde,* line 90, and "tabre ne trompe," *Piers Plowman* C xvi, line 205.

9   *werkmen.* Ritson, Hall, Collette, *weremen.* Wright, Stedman, James and Simons retain *werkmen.*

    walked full wide. See 8.29 and compare "walked full wyde," YP 30.299.

10   *the gudes that thai robbed.* Scholle, *godes.* Like the French citizens of Calais (see the note to 8.1), the Spanish are accused here by Minot of piracy for their depredations on English wine shipments from Bordeaux (see l. 25). Unlike the cowardly French and treacherous Scots, however, the Castilians are for Minot "wight men in were," worthy opponents for Edward's noble warriors, whose ranks included the Black Prince and the ten-year-old John of Gaunt, Sir John Chandos, Henry of Lancaster, and Robert of Namur, who commanded the flagship, *Salle du Roy,* while Edward himself took command of the smaller cog, *Thomas,* so acting out the iconography of the recently minted gold noble (see poem 5, headnote).

    it. Omitted by Ritson, Scholle, and Stedman.

13   *tho.* Wright, *the.*   *wight.* Scholle, *wighte.*   *were.* Scholle, *werre.*

14   *thaire hurdis, thaire ankers.* Tidings of the English fleet gathering at Winchelsea had reached Charles de la Cerda while still in Flanders. He had delayed his departure, fitting out the merchant vessels in the fleet (the tarets) with high wooden castles from which crossbowmen could fire down on the attacking English ships.

    Scholle inserts *and* after *hurdis.*   *here.* Scholle, *herre.*

15   *wight.* Scholle, *wighte.*   *nerr.* Scholle, *nerre.*

17   *Fer might thai noght flit.* See "to flitte full ferre," YP 9.58.

        Scholle inserts *flit* before *thai.*   *Fer.* Scholle, *ferre.*

18   *thai bifore.* Scholle, *bifore thai*; Hall suggests *that thai had bifore reved.*

19   *Boy with thi blac berd.* The reference is to the Genoese sea captain, Julius Boccanera, known also as Barbenoire or Blackbeard. Under Alfonso IX, King of Castile, Boccanera was made Admiral of the Castilian Fleet and created Earl of Parma. Sailing his squadron of thirty Genoese galleys out to sea, he had escaped capture at Sluys in 1340 (see 5.27).

        thou. MS: *tho.* Stedman and Hall, *thou.*

20   *syn.* James and Simons, *sin.*

21   *on.* Hall suggests *opon.*

22   *sall.* Scholle, *sal*, and so 23 and 29.

24   *dye on a day.* A collocation found in fifteenth-century religious lyrics and in the York plays: "I dye this daye," YP 10.257.   *domp.* Scholle, *dump.*

25   *Ye broght out of Bretayne.* In November, 1349, the Castilian fleet had attacked English merchant ships sailing from Bordeaux, killing the crews and commandeering the ships and their cargoes.

26   *marchandes.* Scholle, *marchands.*

27   Scholle, *It es resoun and right that ye evil fare*; Hall notes that "*gude* is superfluous, but *misfare* seems necessary to the rhythm."

28   *new.* Scholle, *newe.*

29   *sir.* Wright, *ser.*

30   *strenkith.* Scholle, *strenkth.* Compare "*he es a strenkithi swayn*," MS 64a[2].

[XI]   **How gentill sir Edward with his grete engines**
wan with his wight men the castell of Gynes.

The taking of Guînes, January, 1352: On 28 September 1347, the Truce of
Calais was signed, which was to last for the following eight years. Three years
later, a week before *Les Espagnols-sur-mer* (poem 10), King Philip of Valois
died and his son, John of France, succeeded him to the throne. A year after
the defeat of the Castilian fleet, a truce was signed with King Pedro of
Castile, which would remain in force until 1372. The rubric for poem 11 is
therefore somewhat misleading, for the ancient castle at Guînes was not
taken with siege engines and force but surrendered to the highest bidder,
Edward. Although King John complained to Edward about truce-breaking,
he certainly suspected treachery, for he had Sir William Beauconray, who had
been the deputy captain of Guînes at the critical moment, torn to pieces by
wild horses. Minot's poem follows generally the English account given by
Geoffrey Le Baker and Robert of Avesbury, with one significant variation
(see line 20, note).

3   *Both the lely and the lipard.* Edward III was the first English King to quarter
the leopards of the Royal Arms of England with the French lily — the fleur-
de-lys. The green here would represent the champ or field of the shield.

4   *Mari, have minde of thi man.* That is, Edward III.

        minde. James and Simons, *mind.*   *whote.* Scholle, *wote.*

5   *mak.* Collete, *make.*

7   *ful.* Collete, *full.*

8   *We wote wele that woning ፡ was wikked for to win.* Some editors have taken the
first person plural as evidence that Minot was present at the capture of the
town. Only six miles from Calais, Guînes was an old-fashioned citadel in the
process of being reinforced. It would undoubtedly have proven difficult to
seize by force.

13   *ful.* omitted by Scholle.   *Gentill John of Doncaster.* An English archer,
reputedly captured by the French and imprisoned at Guînes. The story goes
that he escaped, returned to Calais where he assembled a small force, and re-

entering Guînes via his escape route, surprised the garrison and captured the town. Stedman points out that Doncaster is not too far distant from Minot family estates in Yorkshire.

15   *castell.* Collette, *castel.*

16   *folk that he fand.* Compare "folke that we her fynde," YP 16.156.

17   *Dred.* Collette, *Drede.*

18   *faine war thai to fle.* See 3.70 and compare "schall be full fayne to flee," YP 27.146.

20   *a small bote was tharby.* Here Minot is perhaps more reliable than other accounts that may reflect the influence of a literary *topos.* Chronicles have the moat passable, for the convenience of fishermen, by means of a wall hidden under three feet of water, the location of which was betrayed to John of Doncaster by an enamored French laundress. The reputed treachery of infatuated washerwomen, however, is a commonplace of misogynistic literature and may be traced to a pseudo-Ovidian play, in which a jealous washerwoman conceals the murder of her lover and her rival by betraying the besieged town to the enemy. The play had wide circulation, for it was part of a treatise by John of Garland often used as a school text (see Lawler, p. 139).

24   *Franche men.* Collette, *Franchemen.*

29   *wendes with wo.* See "To wo are we weendande," YP 1.96.

30   *wonen.* Scholle, *wonnen.*   Hall suggests *the* for *tham.*

31   *Ye men of Saint Omers.* Two years earlier, the French captain of St. Omers, Geoffrey de Chargny, had tried to re-take Calais by suborning Edward's Lombard governor, Sir Aymery de Pavie, with 20,000 crowns. The treachery failed, and the French were defeated.

32   *yowre paviliownes.* Robbins suggests the word, generally meaning tents, is here to be understood as "standards" or "banners."

33   Scholle omits *sir.*

34   *es*. James and Simons, *is*.

35   *bede*. Collette, *bide*.

36   MS: *haveves*.

37   Scholle omits *his right*; Hall suggests *God save Edward his right*.

Glossary

This Glossary is based on the Middle English Dictionary through fascicle T and on the glossaries of Hall's edition and Collette's dissertation.

ABATE, *v.* strike or beat down, demolish, 8.19. **abated**, *pp.* 4.64, 5.51; *pt. s.* 7.44. [OF *abatre*.]

ABIDE, *imp. s.* remain, 2.22; **abyde**, halt, stop, 7.42. **habide**, wait for, 1.23, 7.106, 8.31; hold the field, 11.35. **habyde**, 11.34. [OE *abiden*.]

AFFIANCE, *n.* assurance, trust, 7.162. [OF]

AILED, *pp.* troubled, afflicted, harmed, 9.27. [OE *eglian*.]

AIRE, *n.* heir, 4.28. [AF *heir, aire* & L *heres*.]

AL, *adj.* all, 1.16; **all**, 1.18. [OE *al*.]

ALBLAST, *n.* crossbow, arbalast, 4.82. [OF *arbaleste*, L *arcubalista*.]

ALD, *pl.* old people, 3.19. [OE *eldo*.]

ALL, *adv.* quite, altogether, 1.37, 39, 10.30. **all-if**, *conj.* although, 1.85.

ALLANE, *adj.* alone, 9.65. [From phrase *al one*.]

ALS, *conj.* as, 1.5 etc.; *adv.* also, 1.51, *etc.* **alls**, also, 1.60. **also**, 3.51. [OE *alswa*.]

ALWAY, *adv.* ever, 7.62. [OE *ealne weg*.]

ALWELDAND, *ppl.* omnipotent, almighty, all-ruling, 7.26. [OE]

ANE, *pron.* one 3.94. **a**, 9.53.

ANKERS, *pl.* ship's anchors, 10.14. [OE *ancor*, OF *ancre*, & L *anc(h)ora*.]

ANOTHER, *adj.* different, 1.67, 3.72.

ANY, *adj.* limiting adjective, 11.15. [OE *aenig*.]

ARE, *adv.* formerly, before, 7.128, 9.58. [OE *ær* & ON *ar*.]

ARE, *n.* mercy, grace, 8.62. [OE *ar*.]

ARMED, *adj.* equipped for battle, armed, 5.85. [From OF *armer*.]

ARMURE, *n.* weapons and armor, 7.155. [OF *armeure*, from L *armatura*.]

ASCRY, *n.* report, recognizance, 4.40. [AF; cp. CF *escri*.]

ASSEMBLE, *v.* to convene, to gather, 3.43. [*OF assembler*.]

ASSOYL, *v.* absolve, grant remission of sins, 9.30; *pr. s. subj.* 3.115, 7.33. **assoyle**, 5.88. [OF *assoiler*.]

AVAILE, *v.* assist, help, profit, 3.46. [Prob. AF; cp. OF *valoir*.]

AVANCE, *v.* to advance, prosper, 9.5. [OF *avaunc(i)er*.]

AVAUNCE, *v.* to assist, benefit, 1.70.

AX, *n.* ax, 7.84. [OE *æcs, æxa*.]

AY, *adv.* always, 1.63, 3.124. **ay whils**, *conj.* although, 1.28.

BACHILERE, *n.* squire, a knight in the service of another knight, 5.48. [OF *bacheler.*]

BAD, *pt. s.* ordered, 4.34, 6.63. See BID.

BADE, *pt. pl.* offered, 5.55. See BEDE.

BAKEN, *v.* to bake, 9.51. [OE *bacan, boc, bacen.*]

BALDE, *adj.* courageous, fearless, daring, 11.13. [OE *balde, bealde.*] See BOLD(E).

BALDELY, *adv.* bravely, courageously, fearlessly, boldly, 5.55. **baldly,** 3.96, 7.83. [OE *b(e)aldlice.*]

BALE, *n.* grief, 1.4; distress, anguish, 2.28; woe, 6.62, 7.16, 8.20, torment, grief, 10.22. [OE *bealo.*]

BAN, *v.* curse, 8.94 [OE *bannan;* OF *banir.*]

BAND, *n.* bond, feudal obligation, 6.47; **bandes,** *pl.* bands, fetters, 5.73. [=OLG, ON *band.*]

BANER, *n.* the distinctive banner of a lord or country, 1.61, 2.8. [OF *ban(i)ere.*]

BANKES, *n. pl.* natural ridge, 7.21, hills, 8.20. [ON]

BARE, *n.* boar, 6.53, 7.9, 7.42, 7.44, 7.47, 7.52, 7.96, 7.97, 7.106, 7.150, 7.167, 8.19, 8.25, 8.49, 8.87, 9.8. [OE *bar.*]

BARE, *adj.* stripped, empty, 2.20, 7.123, desolate, barren, 5.10, 7.21, 8.20, deprived of, 6.24, 6.25, ruined, 10.26. [OE *baer.*]

BARE, *pp.* suffered, endured, 3.124. [OE *beran.*]

BARELY, *adv.* fully, openly, 8.94.

[From OE *baer.* adj.]

BARGAN, *n.* a business transaction, agreement, 7.64. [OF *bargai(g)ne.*]

BARONS, *n. pl.* members of the nobility, barons, 5.26. **barounes,** 3.43.

BATAIL, *n.* armed conflict, warfare, combat, 5.T1, 7.83; army, 7.22, 8.52. **bataile,** combat, 1.T2, 5.83, 11.35; **bataill,** 8.31; **bataille,** 9.8; **batale,** 4.33; **batayl,** 2.T2, 5.40; **batayle,** 4.78. [OF]

BEDE, *v.* offer, 2.9; present himself, 5.40. **bade,** *pt. pl.* offered, 5.55. [OE *beodan.*]

BELD, *n.* protector, defender, help, 7.27 [A *baeldo,* WS *bieldu.*]

BENDE, *v.* to draw back the string of a bow, 6.23. **bent,** *pp.* 7.84, 7.85, 9.23. [OE *bendan & bend.*]

BENE, *pp.* to be, 4.13; **er,** *pres 3rd pl.* 1.39, 1.63, *etc.*

BENT, *pp.* to draw back the string of a bow; see BENDE.

BERD(E), *n.* facial hair, beard, 4.30, 4.96, 10.19. [OE *beard.*]

BERE, *n.* bier, coffin 6.48, 49. [WS *baer,* A *ber.*]

BEREBAG, *n.* one who caries a bag; contemptuous term for a Scot, 2.20, 9.23. [Cp. *beren* (1) & *bag.*]

BEST, *n. adj. adv.* superlative, best; *adv.* 3.34, *n.* 5.59, *adv.* 7.27, *n.* 7.147, *adj.* 7.158, 164, *n.* 8.65. [OE *betst.*]

BESTES, *n.* an animal, a beast, 1.6. [OF]

BESY, *adj.* engaged in activity, 1.30. [OE *bisig.*]

BETES, *v.* walks or frequents the streets, *pres. 3rd. sg.* 2.25; **betin,** *pp.*

beaten, 2.8. [OE *beatan.*]

BETES, *v.* relieve, remedy, 2.28, 29. [OE *betan.*]

BETTER, *adj.* something or someone superior in quality, 3.40, 3.111, 4.58, 4.86. [OE *betera.*]

BI, *adv.* in phrases of time: during, 7.171, 8.27; in accordance with, according to, 8.40, 8.63. [OE *bi.*]

BICHE, *n.* female dog, bitch, also cur, 8.78. [OE *bicce.*]

BID, *v.* pray, ask, *pres. 1st sg.* 1.3; **bad**, *pt. s.* ordered, 4.34, 6.63. [OE *biddan.*]

BIDE, *v.* to stay, remain, 4.65, 5.52, 6.63. [OE *bidan.*]

BIDENE, *adv.* as an emphatic, or for rime's sake: indeed, 8.74; with a noun or pron., as a group, one and all, all together, 3.77, 8.11. **bydene**, indeed, rime filler. [Only in N and NM texts, always with close e.]

BIFALL, *v.* to come to pass, come about, happen, occur, 3.26. [OE *befeallan.*]

BIFOR, *prep.* in front of, 6.T2, 7.22, 7.49, 7.168, 7.172, 8.T2. **byfor**, 5.27. [OE *beforan.*]

BIFORE, *adv.* at an earlier time, formerly, 1.40, 1.90, 4.14, 10.18. **biforn**, 3.110.

BIG, *adj.* strong, sturdy, robust, 7.83. [origin obscure, cp. Norw. *bugge.*]

BIG, *v.* to build a house, erect, lay out or build a city, 8.26. **bigged**, *pp.* lodged 7.168. **bigges**, *pres. 3rd s.* holds, 8.24. [ON]

BIGILE, *v.* to deceive, delude, beguile, 8.44. [OF *guiler.*]

BIGIN, *v.* to start, to begin, commence, 4.78, 7.13, 20, 30, 10.22, *etc.* **bigyn**, 9.29. **bigins**, 8.25. **bigon**, *pt. s.* 9.49. **bygun**, *pp.* 7.149. [OE *beginnan.*]

BIGING, *n.* a house, building, dwelling, 2.20, 7.123. **biginges**, *pl.* 6.35. [From OE *biggen* v.]

BIKER, *v.* to fight, attack, assult, 5.55, 11.34. [E. Fris. *bikkern*; M. Du. *bicken.*]

BILEVID, *v.* remained, stayed still, 3.66, 7.101. [OE *belæfen.*]

BISIDE, *prep.*, *adv.* near, close by; nearby, at one's side, 7.102, 8.25, 8.28. [OE *bi sidan.*]

BISSCHOPPES, *n.* dignitary of the Christian Church having jurisdiction over a diocese, 3.17, 7.137. [OE *bisc(e)op.*]

BITHOGHT, *v.* considered, pondered, 3.47; devised, planned, 6.55; well-informed, thoughtful, 7.111. [OE *beþencan.*]

BITID, *v.* to happen, to come to pass, 1.73. **bityde**, befall, afflict, 2.12. [From *tiden* (OE *tidan*).]

BITWIXEN, *adv.* of location or position in space, between, 7.134. [OE *betwix.*]

BLAC, *adj.* the color black, 10.19. [OE *blæc.*]

BLAME, *v.* to be guilty of, to be at fault, 1.62; to be criticized, 5.15. [OF *bla(s)mer.*]

BLAME, *n.* guilt, charge, accusation, 3.124. [OF *bla(s)me.*]

BLAN, *v.* stopped, 7.T2. See BLIN

BLAW, *v.* to sound a trumpet, blow a

horn, 4.80. [OE *blawan*.]

BLEDE, *v.* to bleed, 7.52, 53. [OE *bledan*.]

BLIN, *v.* to cease, cause to cease, 5.86, 9.31, 10.19; to stop moving, 6.72. **blinned**, *past 3rd sg.* ceased, 5.87. **blan**, *past 3rd sg.* stopped, 7.T2. [OE *blinnan*.]

BLIS, *v.* to bless, 3.126. [OE *gebletsian*.]

BLIS, *n.* blessedness, 3.114; joy, 6.24, 6.25, 7.167, 8.19. [OE *bliss*.]

BLITH, *adj.* joyful, glad, happy, 7.128, 8.49. [OE *bliþe*.]

BODY, *n.* physical self or being, 3.3, 3.66, 5.40. [OE *bodig*.]

BOGHT, *v.* acquired, 1.43; to suffer for, pay for, 3.119, 7.64. [OE *bycgan*.]

BOKES, *n.* books, 7.3, 6. [OE *boc*.]

BOLD(E), *adj.* courageous, fearless, daring, 4.68, 4.76, 5.40, 7.53, 7.85. [A *bald*, WS *beald*.]

BOLDMEN, *n.* stout fellows, 5.54.

BONE, *n.* prayer, request, 1.3, 4.46. [ON]

BORE, *n.* an uncastrated male swine, a boar, 6.3, 7.21, 11.34. See BARE.

BORN, *v.* to overthrow, suppress in *born all doune*, 1.61; to be born, give birth to, 3.109, 8.12. [OE *beran*.]

BOST(E), *n.* a boast or boastful speech, a meancing threat, 1.18, 62, 2.8, 20, 4.66, 5.50, 51, 86, 87, 6.26, 8.85. **bosting**, *ger.* 2.9. [AF *bost*.]

BOT, *conj.* but, 1.47, 2.16, 18, *etc.*; as *prep.* except, 2.18; as *adv.* only, 8.45.

BOTE, *n.* remedy, relief, reward, 4.58, 6.26. **bute**, 1.4, 5.6. [OE *bot*, acc. *bote*.]

BOTE, *n.* boat, 11.20. **botes**, *pl.* 3.82. [OE *bat*, pl. *batas*.]

BOUN(E), *adj.* ready, eager, willing, prepared, 1.63, 2.9, 11.34. [OI *buin*.]

BOURE, *n.* bower, dwelling, shelter, 8.26. [OE *bur*.]

BOW, *n.* a long-bow, cross-bow, 3.96, 4.82, 9.23; **bowes**, 5.54, 6.23, 7.84, 7.85. [OE *boga*.]

BOY, *n.* ordinary fellow, foot soldier, person of low degree, 10.19. [OF *em)buie, em)boie*.]

BRADE, *adj.* wide, broad, large, 5.54, 7.84. [OE *brad*.]

BRAK, *pt. pl.* broke, 7.78. See BREKE.

BRANDES, *n.* brands, torches, flames, 7.70. [OE *brond*.]

BREDE, *n.* bread, 9.51. [OE *bread*.]

BREKE, *v.* break, destroy, 6.36; **brak**, *pt. pl.* broke, 7.78. [OE *brecan*.]

BREN(E), *v.* burn, 6.35, 7.89. **brend**, *pt. pl.* burned, 3.61. **brin**, burn, 3.55, 5.10. [OE *biernan*.]

BRENIS, *n.* a coat of mail, corselet, 6.3. [OI *brynja*, OF *brunie*, OE *byrne*.]

BRERE, *n.* plant with thorns, briar, bush, 7.128. [OE *brær*.]

BREST, *n.* chest, 7.22. [OE *breost*.]

BRID, n. a young woman, maiden, 1.79. [OE *bryd*, cp. *birde*.]

BRID, *n.* bird, 7.128. [OE *brid*.]

BRIG, *n.* bridge, 7.78. [OE *brycge*.]

BRIGHT, *adj.* bright, brilliant, 5.29, 6.3. [OA *breht*, WS *beorht*.]

BRIM, *n.* a body of water, sea, 5.57. [OE]

BRIN, *v.* burn, 3.55, 5.10. See

BREN(E).

BRING, *v.* to bring, give, raise, 3.48, 114, 5.6, 6.47, 8.68; **broght**, 2.36, 4.37, 66, 5.48, 50, 54, 73, 6.4, 48, *etc.* [OE *bringen.*]

BUD, *v.* to be constrained, obliged, required, (Northern form past plural used impersonally) 5.52, 9.28. [OE *behovan, behefe.*]

BUKLER, *n.* a small shield, 5.34. [OE *bocler.*]

BURGASE, *n.* townsfolk, citisens, 8.65; **buriase**, *pl.* 5.15. [OF *burgeis, borgeis.*]

BUSK, *v.* to hasten, make ready, hurry, (used impersonally) 2.22. [OI *buask.*]

BUTE, *n.* remedy, relief, 1.4, 5.6. See BOTE.

BY, *adv.* of time, of means, 1.34, 4.30, 5.17; *prep.* of location, direction, 5.46, 8.24, 11.33. [OE *by.*]

BYDENE, *adv.* as an emphatic, or for rime's sake: indeed, rime filler. See BIDENE.

BYFOR, *prep.* in front of, 5.27. See BIFOR.

BYGUN, *v.* begin, commence, *pp.* 7.149. See BIGIN.

CAITEFES, *n.* a miserable person, a wretch, a scoundrel, 1.75, 5.58. [AF *caitif.*]

CALL, *v.* to summon, call to a place, 7.112. [ON; cp. OI *kalla.*]

CANT, *adj.* bold, brave, fierce, 7.107. [Cp. MDu. *kant.*]

CANTLY, *adv.* boldly, vigorously, 5.64. [From *cant* adj.]

CARDINALES, *n.* a cardinal, an eminent churchman, 8.40, 41. [L *cardinalis.*]

CARE, *n.* sorrow, sadness, grief; also, annoyance, vexation, 1.11, 2.10, 19, 5.7, 6.18, 39, 7.120, 8.8, 9.60, 10.25, 11.26; the pain of disease or death, 4.90, 7.87, 10.23. [OE *caru, cearu.*]

CARE, *v.* care, worry, 8.1. [OE *carian, cearian.*]

CAST, *v. fig.* bring into a state, a condition, 5.7, 6.18; overpowered, defeated, 7.159. **kast**, bring into a state, 9.60. **casten**, thrown, 5.57. [ON]

CASTELL, *n.* a castle; also, a fortress, a fortified place, 11.T2, 15; **kastell**, 11.11, 30. [OE & AF *castel*, L *castellum.*]

CAT, *n.* a domesticated cat, 8.75. [OE *cat, catte* & OF *chat.*]

CATAILE, goods, propety, 9.26; **catell**, 7.124, 126. [AF; cp. CF *chatel.*]

CHANCE, *n.* something that happens or takes place, an occurrence or event, 1.72; **chaunce**, 1.73. [OF *chea(u)nce, keanche, chance.*]

CHERE, *n.* frame of mind, state of feeling, spirit, mood, 4.45. [OF *chiere, chere.*]

CHILDE, *n.* a boy or girl, 3.56. [OE *cild.*]

CHIN, *n.* the bone of the lower jaw, 5.85. [OE *cin(n).*]

CLENE, *adv.* completely, fully, wholly, altogether, entirely, 8.77. [OE *clæne.*]

CLERE, *adj.* Of weather, sky: not stormy, mild, fair, 4.48. [OF]

CLERK, *n.* one who is educated; a

learned person, scholar, 7.2. **clerkes**, *pl.*
7.4, 9.14. [OE *clerc, cleric* & OF *clerc,*
L *clericus.*]

CLIP, *v.* to embrace, 6.29. [OE
clyppan.]

COLDE, *adv.* coldly; unfeelingly;
distressingly, 4.67, 7.87. [From *adj.*]

COME, *v. past 3rd sg. & pl.* arrive,
approach, 3.86, 21, 60, 107, 4.94, 5.82,
27, 6.70, 7.51, 95, 8.60, 66, 10.6, 11.14.
comen, *pp.* 5.64; come, went, 3.T;
appeared, 5.60; left, departed from,
5.58. See CUM.

COMUN, *adj.* pertaining to, affecting,
or open to, all the people of a
community or class; as *n.* the people,
citizenry, 8.67. [OF *com(m)une* & L
commun-is.]

CONFORT, *n.* encouragement;
courage, assurance, trust, 1.83, 4.47.
[OF]

CONIG, *n.* a rabbit, 8.75. [OF *conin* &
conis.]

COROUN, *n.* a monarch's crown, 9.46.
[OF *corone, corune, curune* & L
corona.]

COSTE, *n.* shore, coast, 7.38, 10.22.
[OF]

COUNSAIL(E), *n.* a meeting,
conference, council, 7.112; counsel,
advice, consultation, 3.45, 8.40, 43. [OF
concile, conseil.]

COVAITISE, *n.* immoderate desire for
acquiring worldly goods or estate;
covetousness, greed, 9.26. [OF
coveitise, covoitise.]

COWARD, *n.* a coward, recreant,
despicable person, 4.90, 5.11. [OF

co(u)arde.]

CRAFT, *n.* a trade, an occupation, 5.69.
[WS, Nhb. *cræft* & Merc. Kt. *-creft.*]

CRAK, *v.* to break in two; to split
someone's head open, 2.10. **crakked** *pp.*
1.59, 2.11. [OE *cracian.*]

CREDE, *n.* in *fig.* and proverbial
expressions: teach a lesson, punish, 8.4,
9.38, 11.14. [[OE *creda*; ult. L.]

CRI, *v.* to lament, demand, beg,
entreat, 1.69. **cried**, *past 3rd pl.* 8.62.
[OF *crier, criier.*]

CROS(S), *n.* the cross of Christ, an
outdoor or roadside cross, 9.T2, 28, 64.
[OE *cros.*]

CROUNE, *n.* a monarch's crown,
7.170; the top of the head, crown,
skull, 2.11. See COROUN.

CROWNE, *n.* the top of the head,
crown, skull, 1.59, 2.10. See COROUN.

CUM, *v.* approach, 4.42, 10.22. **cumes**,
pres. 3rd pl. 6.43; **cum**, proceed from,
7.9; arrive (at), 8.91. **cumes** 6.50. [OE
cuman.]

CUMAND, *v.* to give an order, to
request, 3.53 [OF *comander.*]

CUMANDMENT, *n.* an order, request,
or instruction, 3.50. [OF]

CUMBERD, *v. pp.* loaded, burdened,
7.120. [OF *combrer.*]

CUMEN, *v.* arrive (at) 3.11, 4.29, 8.8,
87, 9.54. See CUM.

CUMLY, adj. & *n.* of appearance:
handsome, stately; of noble birth
and/or bearing, 4.1, 3. See KUMLY.
[From OE *cymlic.*]

CUMPANY, n. a body of followers,
attendants, retainers, 4.21. [OF

compa(i)gnie.]

CUNTRE, *n.* any politically organized area: realm, domain, country, province, 4.28. [OF *contrée, cuntrede.*]

CURSED, *v. pp.* misc. senses: abominable, detestable; malicious, 1.75. [OE *cursian.*]

CUSTOM, *n.* traditional or customary practice of a nation or group, 5.79; a customary rent, service, a tribute tax, 10.25. [OF *costume, custume.*]

DAIS, *n.* the light part of a natural day, daytime, 7.171. See DAY.

DALE, *n. fig.* world, place, 1.8, 9; a pit or grave, 10.3. [OE *dæl.*]

DANCE, *n. fig.* ironic for battle, 7.58; situation, 8.72. See DAUNCE.

DAR, *v.* to have the courage to do something, dare, 8.31, 11.34, 35; **durst**, *past 3rd sg. & pl.* 1.23, 25, 4.42, 65, 7.106, 140. [OE *durran.*]

DARE, to be dismayed, dispirited, scared, 1.9; **dareand**, 1.39. [OE *darian.*]

DAUNCE, *n.* an activity or affair, 1.66, 7.148, 149; a lesson, 5.14, situation or predicament, 7.74. [OF]

DAUNCE, *v.* to move about, 9.3; **daunced**, dance to music, 5.29. [OF *dauncer.*]

DAY, *n.* the light part of a natural day, daytime, 1.34, 3.9, 27, 103, 7.114, 8.39; point of time, present, 3.39, 10.24; day of judgement, 6.7; **dayes**, point of time, present, 4.32. [OE *dæg*, pl. *dagas.*]

DED, *adj.* futile, 10.3. [OE *dead.*]

DEDE, *n.* an action, a deed; an heroic deed, military achievement, 1.23, 52,

3.92, 5.82, 9.39, 10.3, 11.13; **dedes**, 1.8, 10. [OE: A *ded*, K *ded*, WS *dæd.*]

DED, *n.* dying, death, 8.15, 10.3; **dede**, 6.68; **dedes**, 1.26. [Blend of OE *deað* n. & *dead* adj.]

DEFENDES, *v.* to fight in defense of, defend by fighting, 3.7. [OF *defendre* & L *defendere.*]

DELAY, *n.* postponement, delay; immediately, 4.35. [OF]

DELE, n. (2), a large part of something, 3.38. [OE *dæl*, pl. *dælas.*]

DELID, *v.* to deliver a blow or blows, 7.141; **delt**, 7.98. [OE *dæan.*]

DENE, *n.* a place of refuge, a hiding place, 6.33. [MHG *denne.*]

DEPE, *n.* deep water, sea, 10.24. [OE *deope.*]

DERE, *n.* harm, injury, wound, 1.10. [OE *daru.*]

DERE, *v.* to injure, harm, damage, 1.52, 8.10. [OE *derian.*]

DERE, *adj.* costly, expensive, precious, 7.126. [OE *deore.*]

DERE, *adv.* dearly, costly. 1.43, 3.119, 7.64. [OE *deore.*]

DERN, *adj.* stealthy, insidious, crafty; dishonest, secret, 1.10. [OA *derne*, WS *dierne, dyrne.*]

DESPITE, *n.* a feeling or attitude of contempt, disdain, or haughtiness; also, ill will, malice, hostility, scorn, 7.122. [OF]

DID, *v. emphatic*, 1.78, *past 3rd* sg & *pl.* performed, 3.123, 11.13; caused, 4.62, 5.45, 56, 8.84. See DO.

DIGHT, *v.* appointed, destined, 1.80, 6.7; to make preparation, prepared, to

Glossary

be ready, 5.25, 41, 7.93, 8.34, 11.22.
dightes, 7.36. [OE *dihtan*.]
DIN, *n.* shouting, uproar; lamentation,
5.84. [OE *dyne*.]
DINE, *v.* to eat, to feed, 11.22, 23. [OF
disner, diner.]
DINER, *n.* the first big meal of the day
(usually eaten at some time between
nine A.M. and noon), 11.22. [OF
disner, disnier, diner.]
DINT, *n.* the blow of a weapon; stroke
of a sword or lance, 1.26, 7.141. **dintes**,
6.34. [OE *dynt*.]
DISTANCE, *n.* hostility, enmity,
disagreement, discord; *idiom*: to ben at
(in) distance, 9.1. [OF *destance*.]
DO, *v.* perform, effect, 3.9, 8.63; cause,
10.24. [OE *don, gedon*.]
DOGHTY, *adj. & n.* bold, brave,
valiant, strong in battle, 3.92;
esteemed, 4.77; excellent, worthy,
honorable, 4.53. [OE *dohtig & dyhtig*.]
DOLE, *n.* sorrow, distress, grief, 1.80,
8.10. [OF *duel*.]
DOLE, *n.* a share; (one's) due share,
lot, 7.140. [OE *dal, gedal*.]
DOLEFUL, *adj.* full of sorrow, sad,
sorrowful, distressed, 8.73. [From *dol*,
n. (2).]
DOMES DAY, *n.* the Last Judgement,
6.7. [OE *dom & daeg*.]
DOMP, *v.* to fall suddenly or headlong,
plunge, 10.24. [ON]
DONE, *v.* to commit sin, wrong, crime,
1.10; completed, finished, at an end,
1.66, 9.8; ruined, 2.24. See DO.
DONGEN, *v.* with *adv.* to knock down;
also, overcome, vanquish; batter down,

7.74. **dongyn**, destroyed, 7.148. [Prob.
OE **dingan*; cp. OE *dencgan* & OI
dengja.]
DOSE, *v.* to perform an action, 8.21.
See DO.
DOUN(E), *adv.* with verbs implying
motion: to a lower place, down,
downward, 7.74, 159. [OE *dune* & *a-
dun(e)*.]
DOUT, *n.* anxiety; fear, fright, 1.26,
2.14, 4.88, 9.63. [OF *dote, doute*.]
DOWTE, *v.* to be anxious, fearful,
6.34. **douted**, be uncertain, fearful,
suspicious, 1.86. [OF *doter, douter*.]
DRANK, *v. past 3rd pl.* drank the
contents of, partook of, 9.44. [OE
drincan.]
DRAY, *n.* noise, confusion, trouble,
tumult, 8.34. [OF *de(s)rei*.]
DRED(E), *n.* fear, fright, terror, 1.39,
9.36, 11.16, 17, 36. [From OE *dreden*
v.]
DRESCE, *v.* to correct a fault, redress
an injury, 1.8. [OF *drecier*.]
DREWRIS, *n.* anything highly prized,
treasure, 7.126. [OF *druerie*.]
DRINK, *n.* a beverage, drink, 4.85.
[OE *drinc, drinca*.]
DRIVE, *v.* fig. from hunting: to chase,
pursue, 5.41; **driven**, to subject
someone to something, 10.3. [OE
drifan.]
DROUPE, *v.* to be downcast, be sad,
grieve, mourn, 1.9. [ON]
DUBBED, *v.* to make a knight, confer
knighthood on, 7.58. [OE *dubbian* &
OF *adober, abouber, adub(b)er*.]
DUC, *n.* a hereditary noble of the

highest rank, 4.22, 5.41. [OF *duc* & L *dux*.]

DUCHE, *adj.* German, 3.20. [MDu. *Duutsch*.]

DUGHTY, *adj.* brave, valiant, 9.39. See DOGHTY.

DUKE, *n.* a hereditary noble of the highest rank, 3.25, 30, 6.61; **dukes**, 4.77. See DUC.

DURST, *v. past 3rd sg. & pl.* to have the courage to do something, dare, 1.23, 25, 4.42, 65, 7.106, 140. See DAR.

DWELL, *v.* to remain, reside, abide, sojourn, 3.12, 4.5, 56, 5.21, 7.36; to continue steadfastly, 1.70, 11.23; to remain dead on the field, 9.8; to suffer, 1.80; **dwelled**, remained, 1.81, 7.37. [OE *dwellan*.]

DWELLING, *n.* place of residence, 2.24. See DWELL.

DY(E), *v.* to cease living, die, 4.24, 10.24. [OI *deyja*.]

EB, *n.* the flowing back, or ebbing, of tidal water, ebb-tide, 5.33. [OE *ebba*.]

EFTER, *adv.* next, thereupon, 3.49, 5.31; *prep.* in search of, 11.33. [OE *eft*, *æft*.]

EGHEN, *n.* the organ of vision, the eyes, 7.92; **ine**, 7.79. [OE *eage*, pl. *eagan*.]

ELS, *adv.* as an alternative, another possibility, 7.115. [OI *ella*.]

END, *n.* one of the two extremities or ends, 9.3. [OE *ende*.]

ENDING, *n.* the act of dying; death, 11.40. [OE *ende*.]

ENGINES, *n.* a machine or structure used in assaulting fortifications, 11.T1. [OF *engin*, *engien*; L *ingenium*.]

ENMYS, *n.* a member of a hostile armed body in war, 1.46. [OF *enemi*, *anemi*.]

ENTRED, *v.* to enter into a confined space or situation, 7.35. [OF *entrer*.]

ER, *v. 2 pr. pl. & 3 pr. pl.* of to be; are, 1.39, 63, 75, 80, 2.6, 6.11, *etc.*

ERE, *n.* the ear as the organ of hearing, ear, 3.86. [OE *eare*.]

ERLE, *n.* any noble ranking below emperor, king, prince, or duke, 1.42, 5.37, 53; **erles**, 5.26. [OE *eorl*.]

ERSBISSCHOP, *n.* archbishop of the Roman Church, 9.29. [OE *ercebiscop*, *ærce-*.]

ERT, *v. 2 pr. s.* of to be; art, 1.4.

ERTOU, *v.* from to be; art thou, 7.124, 125.

ES, *v. pr. s. & pl.* of to be; is, are, 1.17, 55, 5.36, etc.

ETH, *adv.* easily, readily, 5.47. [OE *eaþ(e & ieþ, eþ*.]

ETIN, *v.* partaking of food, eaten, 8.74, 76, 77. [From *eten*.]

EVER, *adv.* of a continuous state or action: always, ever, 1.86, 2.18. [OE *æfre*.]

EVERMARE, *adv.* at all times, on all occasions; forever, eternally, 8.64; **evermore**, 7.154. [OE *æfre ma*.]

EVIL(L), *adv.* evilly, ill, 10.27; **evyll**, 9.59. [OE *yf(e)le*.]

EVYN, *adv.* even, 1.68. [OE *efen*, *efne*.]

FADER, *n.* applied to God: as man's spiritual father in heaven, 7.28. [OE *fæder*.]

FAGHT, *v. past 3rd sg.* to contend with weapons, engage in armed conflict, 5.78, 8.48. See FIGHT.

FAILED, *v.* to be unsuccessful in accomplishing a purpose, realizing a hope, 1.38. [OF *faillir, falir*.]

FAIN(E), *adj*, to be joyful, glad, or happy, desirous of, or eager for, 3.70, 6.58, 11.18, 21. [OE *fæʒ(e)nian*.]

FAIRE, *adj*. pleasing to the sight; beautiful, 6.6, 8.73, 9.6, 40; desirable, 9.46. [OE *fæger*.]

FAIRE, *n*. beautiful or attractive thing, 5.78. [Partly from OE *fæger, n*., partly from *fæger, adj*.]

FAIRE, *adv*. fairly, completely, fully, 4.71, 7.75; auspiciously, beautifully, 5.60; courteously, honorably, 7.116. [OE *fægre*.]

FAITHFULEST, *adj*. loyal, true, trustworthy, 7.161. [AF *feid & fei, fai* (from L *fidem*).]

FALL, *v*. befall, 5.78; to descend, suffer misfortune, 6.30; to be allowed to come to pass, to lapse, 7.115; **fallen**, *pp*. brought down, descended, 9.6, 7. [OE *feallan, afeallan*.]

FALS, *adj*. of persons, given to the practice of deception; deceitful, full of guile; also, guilty of breach of trust, faithless, disloyal, cruel, 1.74, 2.21, 5.23, 7.62, 72, 150, 9.59. [L *fals-um*, OF *fals, faus*.]

FALSHEDE, *n*. deceitfulness, infidelity, disloyalty, 9.61. [From *adj*.]

FAMEN, *n*. a member of a hostile armed band in war; a personal enemy,

6.73, 7.39. [OE *fah-mon, gefah-mon*.]

FAND(E), *v. past 3rd sg. & pl.* look for, seek, discover, 3.93, 6.45, 7.39, 49, 9.43, 11.16, 17, 21. See FIND.

FARE, *n*. a manner of proceeding, acting, or appearing; behavior, conduct, course of action, 1.25, 6.20, 7.118, 11.18; vaunting, 1.24, 10.5. [OE *faru, fær*.]

FARE, *v*. to go from one place to another, 2.21, 4.17, 5.8, 7.116, 8.18, 10.27; to get along, fare, exist, 9.59, 11.25; **fars**, prospers, 3.40; **ferd**, went, 4.19. [OE *faran*.]

FAST, *adv*. earnestly, 1.69, 2.27; vigorously, 3.7, 61, 103; quickly, 4.17, 27, 9.49. [OE *fæste, feste*.]

FAT, *adj*. plentifully filled-out; plump, not lean, 8.73. [OE *fæt*.]

FAYLED, *v. past 3rd sg.* was missing, absent, 9.54. See FAILED.

FEDE, *v*. to serve as food or nourishment, 10.4, 5. [OE *fedan*.]

FELAWS, *n*. companion, associate, acquaintance, 7.135. [ON *felau*.]

FELD(E), *n*. relatively flat open country; a plain, 3.29, 4.49, 56, 74. [OE *feld*.]

FELE, *indef. num.* as *n*., many; as *adj*., many, much, 3.17, 10.5. [OE *fela, feolo, -u, -a, feala* (not inflected).]

FELL, *v*. of weather or of darkness, to come down, descend, 4.43; to cut down, 7.86. See FALL.

FELL, *adj*. treacherous, deceitful, false, guileful, crafty; fierce in combat, 1.74, 5.23, 7.39, 8.33, 9.7. [OF *fel*.]

FELONY, *n*. treachery, betrayal;

deceit, 7.40. [OF *felonie, felunie, felenie.*]

FEN, *n.* marshland; swamp, slough, 3.29. [OE *fen(n.*]

FER, *adj.* distant, far away, 1.56, 3.73; *adv.* at a distance, far, 8.18, 10.17. [OE *feor(r.*]

FERD, *v. past 3rd sg.* went, 4.19. See FARE.

FERD, *v.* to frighten, terrify; to fear something, 4.61, 8.93. See FERE.

FERD(E), *n.* the emotion of fear; the state of being afraid, 4.27, 93, 7.90. [Prob. from the phrase *for fer(e)d.*]

FERE, *n.* companion; an armed supporter, 6.46. [OE *gefera, fera, foera.*]

FERE, *v.* to frighten, terrify; to fear something, 7.69. [OE *gefæren.*]

FERENE, *n.* a fern; esp., bracken, 4.71. [OE *fearn.*]

FERR, *comp. adv.* further, 10.16, 17. See FER.

FERRUM, *adv.* only in phrase *on (o, of, fro) ferrom*: from afar, from a distance, 7.70, 89. [From *ferren, adv.*]

FERS, *adj.* ferocious, violent, cruel; wild, 8.33, 9.7. [L *ferus.*]

FEW, *adj.* small in number, not many, 5.44, 6.19. [OE *feawe.*]

FIGHT, *n.* a hostile engagement between opposing forces, a battle, 3.111. [OE *feoht(e, gefeoht.*]

FIGHT, *v.* to contend with weapons, engage in armed conflict, 1.25, 4.54, 84, 8.36. See FAGHT, FOGHT. [OE *feohtan.*]

FILE, *n.* a worthless person, a base

fellow; a wretch or rascal, a coward, 7.139, 8.47. [Cp. OI *fyla,* OF *fille (de vie).*]

FILL, *n.* an amount sufficient to satisfy need or desire, 5.62, 9.20. [OE *fyll.*]

FIND, *v.* to come upon, discover, learn of, 5.46, 6.19, 7.6; **findes,** *pres. 2nd. sg.* 2.28. See also FAND(E), FUN, FUNDEN. [OE *findan.*]

FINE, *v.* come to an end, die, 10.17. [OF *finer.*]

FIRE, *n.* fire, 7.68, 69. [OE *fyr.*]

FIRST, *ord. num.* as *adj. & n.* first in a sequence, earliest, 1.12, 3.25, 9.44. [OE *fyrst.*]

FISSCHES, *n.* any animal that lives in the water (as distinct from "beast" and "bird"), 10.4, 5. [OE *fisc; pl. fiscas, fixas.*]

FIVE, *card. num.* five, 1.91. [OE *fif.*]

FLAY, *v.* to put to flight, drive away, pursue; to rout or defeat, 9.17. [WS *aflygen* (causitive of *fleon*).]

FLE, *v.* to retreat, run away, flee, 3.70, 4.60, 5.52, 7.10, 11.18. **fleand,** *pr. ppl.* 7.90, **fled,** *past 3rd sg. & pl.* 1.23, 4.27, 88, 93, 7.140, 8.48, 51, 80. [OE *fleon, flion.*]

FLEMID, *v.* to expel, to put to flight, drive away, to go into exile, 1.44. [A *gefleman,* WS *geflieman.*]

FLESCH, *n.* the flesh of an animal, meat, 1.20. [OE *flæsc.*]

FLIT, *v.* to flee or escape (from something), 10.17. [ON; cp. OI *flytja.*]

FLODE, *n.* the sea, 3.83, 121, 5.46, 56. See also FLUDE. [OE *flod.*]

FLOURE, *n.* the blossom of a plant,

flower, 4.25; **flowre**, *fig.* of persons, the promise or expectation of achievement; the best, 4.91. **floures**, 9.7; **flowres**, 9.6. [OF *flour, flor, flur*.]

FLUDE, *n.* the sea, 3.76, 5.78. See FLODE.

FLYE, *n.* fly, bug, flea, 1.24. [OE *fleah*.]

FLYE, *v.* to move or pass through the atmosphere or the sky, 7.70. [OE *fleogan*.]

FO, *n.* a member of a hostile armed body in war, enemies, 9.17. [OE *gefa, gefan*.]

FODE, *n.* a young man, esp., a young warrior, 6.71. [Prob. from OE *foda* as "one who is nursed."]

FOGHTEN, *v. past part.* to do battle, 5.62. See FIGHT.

FOLD, *n.* the earth, the world, land, 8.18. [OE *folde*.]

FOLK, *n.* people, persons, 4.37, 6.30, 7.16, 49, 69, 72, 90. [OE *folc*.]

FONDE, *v.* to try, to attempt, 9.9. [OE *fandian, gefandian*.]

FONE, *num.* not many, few, 2.28, 5.45; **fune**, 2.29. [N blend of *whon* (OE *hwon*) & ME *feue*.]

FOR, *prep.* because of, on account of, in spite of, for as long as, in order to, 1.4, 10, 25, 38, 39, *etc.*

FORBERE, *v.* to restrain, 8.12. [OE *forberan*.]

FORGAT, *v.* to fail to remember, to forget or disregard, 7.67. [A *forge(o)tan*, WS *forgitan*.]

FORGONE, *v.* to forfeit, to lose through wrong-doing, 9.46. [OE *forgan*.]

FORLORE, *v.* to lose (something) completely or irrevocably, 7.59. [OE *forleosan*.]

FORSAID, *v. past part.* aforementioned, 1.57. [From OE *segcan*.]

FORSWORN, *v.* in proverbial expressions: perjured, having sworn falsely, false, 2.21. [OE *forswerian*.]

FORTHI, *pronominal adv. & conj.* for that, on that account, therefore, consequently, 7.75. [OE *forþy*.]

FORWARD, *n.* agreement, compact, treaty, promise, 9.53, 58, 59. [OE *fore-weard*.]

FOTE, *n.* the foot of a man, 4.59, 6.30. [OE *fot*.]

FOUNDED, *v.* to proceed to an action, 1.12. [OE *fundian*.]

FOWLES, *n.* bird, esp. a wild bird, 1.6. [OE *fugol*.]

FRA, *adv.* of place or movement: away, 1.44. [OE *fram, from*.]

FRANCHE, *adj.* pertaining to France or to Frenchmen, 1.13, 7.151, 8.46. [Var. of *Frensh*.]

FRANKIS, *adj.* pertaining to France or the French people, 6.20; **frankisch**, 7.86. [Appar. a blend of *Frenkish* and *Fra(u)nceis*.]

FRE, *adj.* free in rank or condition, noble, aristocratic, 4.10, 29. [OE *freo, frio, frig*.]

FREK, *adj.* eager (to do something), keen, zealous; bold, brave, fierce, 1.13, 4.54, 84. [OE *frec*.]

FRELY, *adj.* freeborn, noble; noble in

character, excellent, 6.71. [OE *freolic*.]

FREND, *n*. a friend, a comrade, an ally, 7.161; **frende**, 6.19; **frendes**, 2.28, 7.75. [OE *freond*.]

FRENDSCHIP, *n*. an amicable relationship between persons; accord, alliance, peace, 6.45, 7.115. [OE *freondscipe*.]

FRERE, *n*. a member of one of the religious mendicant orders, a friar, 7.131. [OE *frere*.]

FRITH, *n*. a park, a woodland, woods, meadow, 3.29. [Orig. prob. distinct from *frith* (1).]

FRO, *adv*. away, back, 1.56, 57, 4.12, 20, 5.16, 68, *etc*. [ON *fra*.]

FUL, *adv*. completely, entirely, sufficiently; as an intensive particle, very, quite, 1.43, 2.31, 3.18, 38, 70, *etc*.; **full**, 3.87, 7.162, 10.9. [OE *ful(l*.]

FUL, *adj*. filled to capacity, 1.76, 2.6, 7.22, 40; **full**, 2.12. [OE *ful(l*.]

FUN, *v. past part*. came upon, encountered, found, 8.93; **funden**, 8.47, 50. See FINDE.

FUNE, *num*. not many, few, 2.29. See FONE.

FURTH, *adv*. of motion or direction: forward, 4.19, 9.25, 47, 10.7. [OE *forþ*.]

FYNE, *v*. cease fighting, come to terms, 11.21. See FINE.

GAF, *v. past 3rd sg. & pl*. gave to, 1.83, 4.85, 5.70. See GIF.

GAI, *adj*. joyous, merry, gay, 1.41. [OF, frm. Gmc.]

GAIN, *v*. obtain, acquire, 1.87. [ON; cp. OI *gegna*.]

GALAY, *n*. a sea-going vessel having both sails and oars, 3.57, 93; **galaies**, 3.51, 97; **galayes**; 3.78; **galays**, 3.79. [OF *galie*.]

GALE, *n*. a way, course; course of action, means, 6.66. [OE **gal*.]

GALIOTES, *n*. a small galley, 3.81. [OF]

GAN, *v*. as a weak auxiliary used with infinitives to form phrases denoting actions or events as occurring: do, did, 1.22, 3.113, 7.69, 9.16, 64, 10.10. [OE *onginnan*.]

GAPIN, *v*. to stare open-mouthed, gape fixedly, 7.135. [OI *gapa*.]

GASE, *v*. to walk, to go, 2.25. [OE *gan*.]

GASTE, *n*. a spiritual being, the Holy Ghost, 4.8. [OE *gast*.]

GAT, *v*. to acquire, earn, buy, win, 5.70. See GET.

GATE, *n*. gate of a city, 7.49, 8.89. [WS *geat*.]

GATE, *n*. a path, road, street; the way from one place to another, 6.54, 7.48, 11.28. [OI *gata*.]

GAUDES, *n*. a fraud, deception, trick, artifice, pretense, 1.87, 2.18, 30. [OF *gaudie*.]

GAY, *adj*. joyous, merry, gay, 1.40. See GAI.

GAYLAYES, *n*. a sea-going vessel, 3.78. See GALAY.

GAYNED, *v*. obtain, acquire, 4.57. See GAIN.

GEDER, *v*. of people: to come together, assemble, congregate, 11.3. [OE *gadrian*.]

GENTILL, *adj.* of noble rank or birth, belonging to the gentry, 7.142, 11.T1, 13. [OF *gentil, jentil.*]

GER, *v.* to prepare or equip (oneself); to make, to cause, bring about, 7.42; **gert**, 3.43, 4.80, 5.86, 6.66, 7.52, 87, 99, 10.16. [OE *gearwian.*]

GESTES, *n.* an invited guest, 11.29. [ON; cp. OI *gestr.*]

GET, *v.* to acquire, earn, buy something, 8.3. [OI *geta.*]

GET, *v.* to watch over, 2.36. [ON *gaeta.*]

GIF, *v.* give to, 5.39, 81, 7.29; **giff**, 4.90; **gifen**, *past part.* 8.88. [OE *gifan.*]

GIFTES, *n.* present, gift, 6.64. [ON *gipt, gift.*]

GILE, *n.* the quality of deceitfulness, dishonesty, treachery, 1.86, 2.6, 12, 18, 24, 30, 36, 7.136. [OF *guile.*]

GLADE, *v.* to gladden; make joyful; also cheer, encourage, 5.54. [OE *gladian.*]

GLADLY, *adv.* with good will, willingly, without hesitation or reluctance, 4.85, 11.7. [OE *glædlice.*]

GLE, *n.* mirth, rejoicing; amusement, pleasure, 3.69, 4.57. [OE *gliw, glig, gleo(w, glio(w, gliu.*]

GOD, *n.* God; God the Father, 1.31, 53. 2.14, 3.1, 58, 108, 109, 114, 115, 4.7, 20, 46, 47, 90, 5.6, 39, 53, 81, 86, 88, 6.75, 80, 7.19, 26, 34, 43, 8.96, 11.37; **goddes**, 3.10. [OE]

GODE, *adj.* good, excellent, 6.80. [OE]

GODE, *n.* possessions, goods, 3.84. [OE]

GOLD, *n.* the metal gold, 6.66, 10.12.

[OE *gold.*]

GRACE, *n.* God's grace, God's gift or favor, 4.8, 7.29; **graces**, 6.80. [OF *grace.*]

GRAME, *n.* grief, sorrow, remorse, vexation, harm, 5.18. [OE *grama.*]

GRANT(E), *v.* to permit, allow; to consent, assent, 3.4, 8, 4.8, 6.80, 8.46. [OF *granter.*]

GRAPES, *n.* a grape, an individual berry of the vine, 4.18. [OF *grape.*]

GRAUNT, *v.* to permit, allow or grant, 6.59. See GRANT(E).

GRAYTHEST, *adj.* ready, available, nearest, 7.48. [ON; cp. OI *greidr.*]

GRENE, *n.* a grassy place, a field, 6.4, 7.102, 11.3; green cloth, 10.12. [OE *grene.*]

GRETE, *adv.* much, a great deal, greatly, 1.11. [OE *great.*]

GRETE, *n.* intrinsically important, famous, 5.80. [OE *great.*]

GRETE, *adj.* large, great, many, 1.6, 3.21, 82, 93, 4.37, 62, 7.2, 41, 8.34, 81, 9.T, 14, 10.5, 11, 11.T1, 18. [OE *great.*]

GRETE, *v.* to greet, welcome, pay one's respects, 11.28; **gretes**, 11.29. [OE *gretan.*]

GRONDE, *n.* the lowest part of something, the bottom, 10.4. [OE *grund.*]

GUDE, *adj.* good, excellent, skilled. adequate, appropriate, 1.83, 2.14, 3.37, 116, 4.47, 5.53, 77, 82, 7.30, 10.27, 11.6, 10. See GODE.

GUDE, *n.* possessions, goods, 3.122, 5.70; **gudes**, 8.11, 14, 10.10. See GODE.

GUDELY, *adv.* graciously, courteously; in a friendly manner, 5.80, 81. [Prob. OE]

GYN, *n.* scheme, strategy, trickery, device, 7.150. [OF *gin.*]

HABIDE, *v.* to wait, be patient; to remain, stay, sojourn, dwell, 1.23, 7.106, 8.31, 11.35; **habyde**, 11.34. [OE *abiden.*]

HALD, *v.* to take hold, grasp, clasp; seize, embrace; to keep from falling; 3.24, 8.37, 11.10; **haldes**, 6.51. [OE; cp. A *haldan.*]

HALELY, *adv.* completely, entirely, 4.92. [From *holle*, adj. 2.]

HALF, *n.* a half part, 5.33. [OE]

HALL, *n.* a large public building, Westminster Hall, 9.11. [OE]

HALY, *adj.* divine, sacred, 1.78, 3.126, 4.8. [OE *halig.*]

HAME, *n.* residence, dwelling, house, 4.89. See HOME.

HAND, *n.* the human hand, 1.21, 6.43, 8.61, 9.30; **handes**, 3.57, 5.72. [OE *hond, hand* & ON]

HANGED, *v.* to suspend, to hang up, 10.14. [OE *hangian.*]

HARDY, *adj.* strong in battle, fearless of danger, 4.68. [OF *hardi, ardi.*]

HARE, *n.* the common European hare, 8.21. [OE *hara.*]

HARM, *n.* loss, ruin, harm, injury; pain, grief, sorrow, 4.95; **harmes**, 2.26, 6.15, 43. [OE *hearm.*]

HASTED, *v.* to hurry, hasten; to drive, push, 4.60, 5.22. [OF *haster.*]

HASTILY, *adv.* speedily, quickly, in a hurry, 3.91, 7.66; **hastly**, 6.44. [From *hast(e* n.]

HAT, *v.* is named, called, 4.74. See HIGHT.

HATE, *v.* to feel hatred for, 6.52. [OE *hatian.*]

HATTES, *n.* an outer head covering, a hat, 8.41. [OE *hæt.*]

HELD, *v.* to take hold, grasp, clasp; seize, embrace; to keep from falling, 3.32, 57, 4.36, 49, 7.171, 8.T2, 9.24, 50. See HALD.

HELE, *v.* to conceal, hide, 6.16; **helis**, 6.17. [OE *helan.*]

HELE, *n.* sound physical condition, health, 11.10. [OE *hælu* & *hæl.*]

HELL, *n.* the Christian hell, place of damnation for evil men, 7.34. [OE *hel* & *helle.*]

HELM, *n.* a helmet, 7.59; **helmis**, 7.105. [OE *helm* & ON]

HELP, *n.* assistance, succour, benefit, 3.107, 9.47. [OE *help* & *helpe* & *hylp.*]

HELP, *v.* to give aid or assistance, provide relief, 1.22, 31, 92, 3.28, 7.19, 8.80; **helpid**, 5.35, 37, 7.100. [OE *helpan.*]

HEND, *n.* the human hand, 3.32. See HAND.

HENDE, *adj.* having the approved courtly or knightly qualities, noble, courtly, well-bred, 7.34. [OE *gehende.*]

HENDE, *adv.* near, close, 6.17. [OE *gehende.*]

HENT, *v.* to take hold of, seize, grasp, 6.15, 9.24. [OE *hentan.*]

HEPE, *n.* a pile, 5.46. [OE *heap.*]

HERD, *v. past 3rd sg.* & *pl.* to hear,

understand, learn of, 3.41, 4.40, 55, 5.19, 8.35. See HERE.

HERE, *adv.* here in this place, 1.65, 5.19, 7.153, 8.25. [OE *here.*]

HERE, *v.* to hear, understand, learn of, 3.50, 6.44; **heres**, 7.169. [OE]

HERE, *adj.* on high, 10.14. See HIGH.

HERIED, *v.* plunder hell, harrow hell, 7.34. [OE *hergian.*]

HERITAGE, *n.* something legally inherited, 4.9, 7.32. [OF *iretage, iritage, h)eritage.*]

HERKINS, *v.* to listen attentively, take heed, harken, 6.T1. [Prob. from *herkenen.*]

HERNES, *n.* the brains of a man or animal, 3.68. [OE *hærnes.*]

HERT, *n.* the heart of a human being or of an animal, 1.11, 21, 6.52, 69, 7.127, 11.17; **hertes**, 3.78, 5.30. [OE *heorte.*]

HETES, *v.* to inspire the heart, the will; to inflame; to vow, to promise, 2.26, 6.51. [OE *hætan.*]

HEVIDDES, *n.* the human head, mind, reason, 4.72; **hevidles**, beheaded, 3.100; **hevyd**, 3.65, 7.59. [OE *heafod.*]

HEVIN, *n.* the abode of God, heaven, paradise, 11.40; **hevyn**, 1.35. [OE *heofon.*]

HIDE, *v.* to conceal, hide, put in a secret place, 1.21, 4.72, 6.16, 8.22, 10.10; **hid**, 1.77; **hided**, 10.11; **hides**, 6.17. [OE *hydan.*]

HIED, *v.* to go quickly, travel rapidly, 4.89. See HYE.

HIGH, *adj.* high, lofty, elevated, 7.166. [WS *heah.*]

HIGHT, *v.* is named, called, 7.2. See HAT.

HILL, *n*, a natural elevation, hill, 1.58. [OE *hyl.*]

HINDE, *adj.* having the approved courtly or knightly qualities, noble, courtly, well-bred, 9.37. See HENDE.

HIRE, *n.* payment for services rendered; reward, compensation, 3.100, 7.66, 8.66. [OE *hyr.*]

HOLE, *n.* a den, cavern; hiding place, 8.22; **holl**, 10.10, 11. [OE *hol.*]

HOMAGE, *n.* to accept a pledge of allegiance from, 3.T2. [OF *omage, hom(m)age, humage.*]

HOME, *n.* residence, dwelling, house, 9.18. [OE *ham.*]

HONOWRE, *n.* fame, good repute, worldly glory, 3.21, 4.92, 9.42. [OF *h)onor, h)onur, onneur.*]

HORS, *n.* a horse, 4.59; **horses**, 8.73. [OE]

HOVED, *v.* to intend something, to purpose something, 3.83, 3.121. [OE *hogian.*]

HOW, *adv.* in what manner or way, 3.T1, 6.T1, 7.T1, 73, 169, 170, 8.T1, 9, 44, *etc.* [OE *hu.*]

HUND, *n.* an ordinary domesticated dog, 8.21; **hundes**, 8.76. [OE *hund.*]

HUNDERETH, *ord. number* from cardinal *hundred*, 3.94; **hundreth**, 3.110, 5.71. [OE]

HUNT, *v.* to pursue, chase, drive; attack, 8.21. [OE *huntian.*]

HURDIS, *n.* a wooden bulwark or other structure on a ship to protect the crew in battle, 10.14. [OF *hordeiz.*]

HYE, *v.* to go quickly, travel rapidly, hasten, 1.22. [OE *higian.*]
HYLL, *n.* a natural elevation, hill, 1.T2. See HILL.

IF, *conj.* introducing a conditional clause: provided that, on condition that, in case that, 1.48, 5.24, 31, 6.60, *etc.* [OE *gif.*]
ILK, *pron.* as *adj.* designating a person, thing, time, place, *etc.*; each, every, 3.89, 7.81; **ilka**, 1.19, 6.12, 11.37; **ilkone**, *pron.* 8.74. [OE *ilca*, *ylca.*]
ILL, *adv.* evilly, wickedly; spitefully, 2.31. [From adj; ON; cp. OI *illr.*]
INE, *n.* organ of vision, eyes, 7.79. See EGHEN.
INES, *n.* lodgings, in phrase **nimen ines**, to procure, find lodgings, 8.27, 9.52. [OE *in.*]
INGLIS, *adj.* pertaining or belonging to England or the English people, 3.95, 101, 106, 124, 5.14, 72, 7.63, 81, 129, 8.10, 11.11; **Inglisch**, 5.T2; **Inglismen**, 7.65; **Ingliss**, 3.112, 7.122. [OE *Englisc*, *ænglisc.*]
INOGH, *adv.* very much, a great deal, sufficiently, 5.9, 7.153. [OE *genog*, *genoh.*]

JAPES, *n.* a trick, deceit, fraud, 4.15. [From *japen* v.]
JORNAY, *n.* any course of action, task, undertaking, 3.40. [OF *jornee*, *jurnee*, *journee.*]
JOY, *n.* the perfect joy of heaven, 3.4. [OF *joi.*]

KAIES, *n.* a key, 8.89; **kayes**, 2.36, 8.88. [OE *cæg.*]
KAITEFS, *n.* a wretch; a scoundrel, 5.58. See CAITEFES.
KAST, *v.* to lower, 9.60. See CAST.
KASTELL, *n.* a castle; also, a fortress, a fortified place, 11.11, 30. See CASTELL.
KAYSER, *n.* title preceding name of a ruler, 3.13. [OE *casere.*]
KEN, *v.* to make known, to give instruction to, teach, 5.87, 6.39, 8.4, 8, 11.14; **kend**, 8.9, 9.38. [OE *cennan.*]
KENE, *adj.* bold, brave, fearless, stalwart, warlike; fierce, savage, cruel, 2.2, 3.78, 4.52, 5.26, 64, 7.107, 8.9, 76, 10.23. [OE *cene.*]
KEPE, *v.* to keep in one's possession; retain, hold, have, 8.90, 10.23, 11.11. [OE *cepan.*]
KEPED, *v.* in the phrase "keped him in the berd"; to attack at close quarters; to meet head-on, 4.96. [OE *cepan.*]
KID, *v. past part.* to make known by speech or writing, 1.75. See KITH.
KINDEL, *v.* to kindle; to incite, stimulate, inflame, stir up, 2.10; **kindels**, 2.19; **kindeld**, 11.26. [Cp. OI *kynda.*]
KING, *n.* a king, monarch, 1.1, 81, 2.4, 3.T1, 2, 11, 85, 90, 4.1, 11, 41, 46, 49, 56, 67, 70, 75, 94, 5.79, 82, 6.T1, 6.71, 7.113, 7.170, 9.12; **kinges**, 3.24, 7.112. [OE *cyning.*]
KIRK, *n.* a consecrated building for Christian worship, church, 1.78. [OE *cir(i)ce.*]

KIRTELL, *n.* a garment for men or boys, usually worn as an outer garment, 8.61. [OE *cyrtel.*]

KITH, *v.* to make known by speech or writing, 5.69. [OE *cyþan.*]

KNAW, *v.* to be aware of as a fact; to be familiar with, 5.47, 7.125. [OE *cnawan.*]

KNELE, *v.* to kneel, fall to the knees, 9.28. [OE *cneowlian.*]

KNIGHT, *n.* a noble warrior; a member of the land-holding ruling class, 4.3, 5.26, 7.95, 8.81; **knightes**, 4.29, 52, 7.57, 9.58. [OE *cniht.*]

KNOK, *v.* to strike, beat, deliver a blow, 7.130; **knoked**, 3.68; **knokked**, 3.65. [OE *cnucian* & *cnocian* & ON]

KNOKKES, *n.* a blow; in pl.: blows, 7.98. [From *knokken, v.*]

KOGGES, *n.* a ship of some kind (apparently of medium size and used in military expeditions) 5.73. [AF *coque, cogge.*]

KOUTH, *v.* to make known by speech or writing, 5.69. See KITH.

KUMLY, *adj.* & *n.* of appearance: handsome, stately; of noble birth and/or bearing, 7.95. See CUMLY.

KUN, *v.* to have ability; be able, capable, 8.90. [OE *cunnan.*]

KYS, *v.* to kiss; to embrace and kiss, 6.29. [OE *cyssan.*]

LADY, *n.* a female sovereign or ruler, the Virgin Mary, 11.5. [OE *hlæfdige.*]

LANCE, *n.* a horseman's spear; also, a throwing spear, javelin, 9.2. [OF *lance.*]

LAND, *n.* a territory considered as a political unit, 1.44, 3.T2, 3.14, 39, 60, 4.4, 23, 6.41, 7.T1, 8.63. See LONDE.

LANG, *adj.* of space, distance; long, extensive, far-reaching, 11.19. [OE *lang.*]

LANG, *adv.* longer, further in time, 3.104. [OE *leng, lencg.*]

LANGER, *adv. comp.* at greater length, longer, 4.16, 65, 5.21, 6.63, 7.80. See LENGER.

LARE, *n.* the action or process of teaching; that which is taught, 5.9, 6.22, 10.28, 29. [OE *lar.*]

LAST, *adj. sup.* latest, last, final, 2.16, 34, 7.67. [Prob. from *adv.*]

LASTED, *v.* to endure, hold out, 3.104. [OE *læstan.*]

LAT, *v.* to grant, allow, leave, permit, 7.115, 8.90. See LETE.

LATE, *adv.* in the latter part of a period of time, late, 6.50, 7.51, 8.91. [OE *late.*]

LAW, *n.* a rule or set of rules prescribing or restraining conduct; law, 8.63. [late OE *lagu.*]

LAW, *adj.* low, 5.50, 7.97, 127, 9.64, 65. [ON *lagr.*]

LAY, *v.* to adopt a recumbent posture, lie down, 3.67, 68; to be deployed, 6.T1. [OE *licgan.*]

LAYKES, *n.* amusement, diversion, game, 3.64. [ON: cp. OI *leikr.*]

LEDDERR, *n.* a ladder, 11.19. [OE *hlæder.*]

LEDE, *v.* to guide, 1.35; to govern, control, 11.39; **ledeing**, command, 8.54. [OE *lædan.*]

LEDERS, *n.* a ruler, lord; a military

commander, 8.94. [OE *lædere*.]

LEFT, *v*. to stop, cease, discontine; to leave, abandon 1.89, 3.38, 5.44, 45, 7.108, 8.71. See LEVED.

LELE, *adj*. loyal, true, faithful; full of prowess, noble, brave, 3.37. [OF *leal*, *leel*.]

LELY, *adv*. faithfully, sincerely; certainly, assuredly, 7.73. [From *lel*, adj.]

LELY, *n*. the plant of the Madonna lily; the French royal insignia, 4.91, 11.3. [OE: from Latin *lilium*.]

LEN, *v*. to grant, give, 11.39. [OE *lænan*.]

LEND, *v*. to stay temporarily, rest, remain, 3.31; **lended**, 8.45. [OE *lendan*.]

LENGER, *adj. comp*. of things, paths: more extended in space, greater in length, longer, 4.35. [OE *lengra*.]

LEPE, *v*. to jump, leap, spring, 5.45, 11.27. [OE *hleapan*.]

LERE, *v*. to teach, give instructions to, 5.58, 6.42, **lered**, 5.14, 34, 8.57, 10.28. [OE *læran*.]

LES, *adv*. in a lower degree, in phrase, never the less, 1.63.

LET, *v*. to hinder, impede, delay, 9.18; **letes**, 9.19; **lett**, halted, 3.64. [OE *lettan*.]

LETE, *v*. to grant, allow, leave, 7.91. [OE]

LETHERIN, *adj*. of leather, leathern, 11.19. [OE *leþer(e)n* & *liþrine*.]

LEVE, *n*. permission, leave; authority or right, 6.61. [OE *leaf* & (late) *gelæfa*.]

LEVE, *v*. to believe in, have faith in, trust, 5.9, 6.22, **leves**, 3.117, 4.73. [OE; cp. A *lefan*.]

LEVED, *v*. to leave, abandon, 9.65; **levid**, 1.55, 8.78. [OE **leafn*.]

LIEN, *v*. to adopt a recumbent posture, lie down, fall prostrate, 7.135; **lies**, 7.127. [OE *licgan*.]

LIF, *v*. to be alive, to live, 4.24, **lifes**, 3.118. [OE; cp. A *lifgan*.]

LIFE, *n*. animate existence, vitality, 3.3, 56, 11.39. [OE *lif*.]

LIG, *v*. to adopt a recumbent posture, lie down, fall prostrate, 7.80, 87; **ligand**, *pres. part*. 8.71; **ligges**, 3.99. See LIEN.

LIGHT, *adj*. cheerful, merry, joyful, 5.30. [OE: cp. A *leht*.]

LIKED, *v. refl*. make happy, please; be pleasing to; wish, choose, 3.34; **likid**, 7.80; **liking**, 5.21. [OE *lician*.]

LINE, *n*. a cord or rope, 11.19. [OF *ligne*.]

LIPARD, *n*. the leopard, 11.3. [OF *liepart*, *leopard*, etc.]

LIST, *adj*. dexterous, adroit; skillful, cunning, 6.43. [OE *list*.]

LIST, *v. impers*. to be pleasing to, 1.71. [OE *lystan*.]

LISTENS, *v*. to listen to; pay heed to, 3.117. [OE *hlystan*.]

LITELL, *adv. & adj*. little, not much, not long, small, short; in a short while, 1.57, 82; **litill**, 4.26, 8.45. [OE *lytel*.]

LITHES, *v*. to listen, be attentive, 1.T1, 5.T1. [ON *hlyda*.]

LIVE, *n*. animate existence, vitality, 1.89; **lives**, 7.143. See LIFE.

LONDE, *n.* a territory considered as a political unit, 9.12. [OE *land, lond.*]

LORD, *n.* the head of a household; the lord of a castle; feudal lord, king, 6.40, 41, 8.63; God, 1.35; **lordes**, 3.31, 44, 4.52. [OE *hlaford.*]

LORN, *v.* to lose, be parted from; to separate from, 4.92. [OE *lesen*; cp. *forleosan.*]

LOSS, *n.* loss in battle or combat, defeat; loss of men in fighting, 9.T1. [OE *los* & ON]

LOUD, *adv.* in the phrase *loud or stille*, under any circumstances, at any time, ever, 8.54. [OE *hlude.*]

LOUT, *v.* to bow, kneel; make obeisance, 6.40, 41, 7.97, 9.64, 10.29; **louted**, 9.65. [OE *lutan.*]

LOVED, *adj.* love, affection or friendship, 1.53. [OE *lufian.*]

LUF, *n.* love, friendship, 7.144. [OE *lufu.*]

LUKED, *v.* in the phrase "luked forth," to look toward, turn one's glance toward. 9.47. [OE *locian.*]

LYE, *n.* a lie, falsehood, 4.73. [OE *lyge.*]

LYE, *v.* to adopt a recumbent posture, lie down, fall prostrate, 7.73. See LIEN.

LYSTENS, *v.* to listen to; pay heed to, 8.57. See LISTENS.

MA, *adj.* greater in number or size, more, 1.42, 48, 49. [OE *mara.*]

MADE, *v. past 3rd sg & pl.* to create; make for, produce; bring about, 1.5, 3.35, 89, 108, 4.46, 81, 5.84, 6.67, 7.97,

123, 9.57, 58. See MAKE.

MAI, MAY, *v.* as aux. with infinitive or denoting ability or capacity, 1.36, 3.10, 5.46, 6.14, 7.27, *etc.* [OE *magan.*]

MAIN, *n.* physical strength, vigor, might, 6.77; **maine**, 1.85. [OE *mægen.*]

MAINTENE, *v.* to help, support; uphold, assist, 1.36, 7.114. [OF *maintenir.*]

MAISTRI, *n.* superior strength, force, violence, 3.113, 7.41. [OF *maistrie.*]

MAK, *v.* to create; make for, produce; bring about, 1.62, 5.10, 6.73, 7.10, 14, 131, 8.87; **make**, 5.1, 7.17, 154; **maked**, 1.49; **makked**, 7.41. [OE *macian.*]

MAN, *n.* a person, a man or a woman, 2.31, 3.36, 55, 89, 5.32, 38, 42, *etc*; **mans**, 11.9. [OE *mann.*]

MANASINGES, *n.* the act of threatening, a threat, menaces, 1.49. [OF *menace, manace, manase.*]

MANE, *n.* lamentation, complaint, 3.108. See MONE.

MANERE, *n.* a way of doing something; method, mode, means, manner, 7.116, 9.55. [OF *maniere.*]

MANI, *adj. & n.* indefinitely numerous, innumerable, great in number, 3.5, 4.3, 5.42, 48, 7.95, 141, 9.23; **many**, 1.51, 59, 79, 2.3, 31, 3.16, *etc.* [OE *manig.*]

MARCHANDES, *n.* a wholesale businessman, a merchant, 10.26. [OF *marcheant* & AF *marchaunt.*]

MARE, *n.* female horse, mare, 8.3, 11.27. [OE *mere.*]

MASE, *v. pres. 3rd pl.* create, make, 8.34. See MAK.

MASTE, *adj. sup. & n.* greatest in

number or quantity; most numerous,
4.7, 7.26. [From *mo* adj. & superlative
suf.; also cp. Nhb *mast*, sup. of *micel*.]
MATER, *n.* business, affair, object of
attention, 7.17. [L *materia* & OF
matiere.]
MAWGRE, *n.* ill-will, displeasure,
shame, 1.50. [OF *maugre*.]
MEDE, *n.* a gift; material reward;
compensation, 1.50, 5.39, 81, 6.70, 7.98,
8.2, 9.40, 11.40. [OE *med*.]
MEKIL, *adj.* great, 5.51, 11.27; **mekill**,
1.85, 3.18, 38, 62, 123, 5.18, *etc.* [OE
micel.]
MEND, *v.* to put right, atone for,
amend, 8.7. [From *amenden*.]
MEND, *v.* to behave, act, 1.29. [OF
demener.]
MENE, *v.* to intend to convey, mean;
intend a certain sense, 11.4, 5; **menid**,
5.1; **ment**, 5.24. [OE *mænan*.]
MENYE, *n.* retinue, retainers,
attendants, host, 1.82, 4.11, 10.T1. [OF
meyné.]
MERCY, *n.* forgiveness, clemency,
4.10. [OF]
MERI, *adj.* cheerful, pleasant, 5.32.
[OE *myrige*.]
MERKES, *n.* in phrases, a desired
object or end, 9.13. [OE *mearc*.]
METE, *n.* meat, edible flesh, food,
4.85. [OE *mete*.]
METE, *v.* to encounter; to come
together, meet, 5.23; **metes**, 2.27; **met**,
1.48, 7.63, 9.4, 10.T2, 10.26; **mett**, 3.63.
[OE *metan*.]
MIDDES, *adv.* in the midst of, 5.56.
[OE *middian*.]

MIDELERD, *n.* earth, 1.5. [OE *middel
ȝeard*.]
MIGHT, *n.* military might; individual
prowess; force, forcefulness, 1.29, 3.8,
4.81, 7.12, 43, 11.27; **mightes**, power,
4.7, 7.26. [OE *miht*.]
MILD, *adj.* merciful, forgiving, 7.43.
[OE *milde* & ON]
MINDE, *n.* individual remembering or
remembrance, 11.4. [OE *gemynd*.]
MINSTER, *n.* Westminster Hall, 9.11.
MIRE, *n.* bog, marsh, swampland, 3.99,
8.71. [ON]
MIRTH, *n.* the feeling of joy or state
of happiness; delight, gladness, 4.81,
8.3; **mirthes**, 6.27. [OE *myrgþ*.]
MIS, *v.* to lack, fail to accomplish,
achieve, understand, 3.113, 6.27;
missed, 9.13; **mys**, 7.119. [OE *missan*.]
MISCHANCE, *n.* a mishap, piece of
bad luck, calamity, 4.20, 8.30, 9.4. [OF
meschëance, -chanse, & ME *mis-* pref.]
MISDEDE, *n.* an offense, a
transgression, misdeed; sin, crime, 8.7.
[OE]
MISFARE, *v.* to fare badly, suffer
misfortune; be defeated in battle,
10.27. [OE *misfaran* & *misferan*.]
MISLIKED, *v.* to be unhappy; be
displeased or dissatisfied, 7.60. [OE
mislician.]
MISLIKING, *n.* displeasure,
indignation, 7.61. [from above.]
MODE, *n.* mind, heart, thought, 6.77.
[OE *mod*.]
MODER, *n.* mother, here, Mother of
God, 4.10. [OE *modor*.]
MODY, *adj.* brave, bold, proud, high-

spirited, courageous, 5.42. [OE *modig.*]

MOLD, *n.* the ground, surface of the earth, 8.3. [OE *molde.*]

MONE, *n.* the moon, 1.5. [OE *mona.*]

MONE, *n.* lament, complaint, 2.27, 9.45, 11.5; **mane**, 3.108. [OE *man.*]

MONÉ, *n.* money, coin, 3.35, 37. [OF *moneie.*]

MORE, *n.* moorland, 9.4. [OE *mor.*]

MORN, *n.* morning, dawn, break of day, 5.31; **mornig**, 4.43. [OE *morgen.*]

MOSTE, *adv.* in the highest degree, 6.70. [OE *mæst.*]

MOTE, *v.* to speak, talk; to dispute, debate, litigate, 6.28. [OE *motian.*]

MOWTH, *n.* the human mouth, 5.1, 7.7. [OE *muþ.*]

MUN, *v.* northern aux. equivalent to shall, should, must, 1.48, 3.119, 6.27, 8.2. [ON *monu.*]

MURNIG, *n.* sorrow, sadness, grief, mourning, 7.119, 8.2. [OE *murnung.*]

MYGHT, *n.* military might; individual prowess; force, forcefulness, strength, 3.112. See MIGHT.

MYLE, *n.* a measure of distance: a mile (denoting any of several variously measured or loosely conceived distances), 1.84, 8.42. [OE *mil.*]

MYS, *v.* to lack; fail to accomplish, achieve, understand, 7.119. See MIS.

MYST, *n.* a weather condition of mist or fog, 4.43. [OE *mist.*]

NAKED, *adj.* not covered with clothing, unclothed; destitute, 1.55. [OE *nacod*, Merc. *næcad.*]

NAKERS, *n.* a small kettledrum, 4.80.

[OF *nacaire* & ML *nacara.*]

NAME, *n.* the name of a human being, 1.58, 5.17, 8.82. [OE *nama.*]

NANE, *pron.* no person; no one, 3.107. See NONE.

NE, *conj.* & *adv.* nor, not, 2.14, 3.110, 4.36, 5.15, 7.100, 109, 121, 8.13, 76, 78, 9.48. [OE *ne.*]

NEDE, *n.* a necessity or need; what is required, wanted, or desired, 5.37, 11.37. [OE]

NEDES, *v.* to be necessary or needful, 3.72, 9.28. [OE *neodan.*]

NEGHED, *v.* to approach, come near (regional), 10.15. [From OE *neah.*]

NERE, *adv.* near in space or time, nearby, close, 4.41, 42; **nerr**, *comp.* nearer in space or time, 10.15. [OE *near.*]

NEVER, *adv.* at no time, never, 1.27, 63, 3.111, 5.62, 7.119, 121, 163, 9.31. [OE *næfre.*]

NEW, *adj.* of recent origin, new, 5.14, 10.28; *adv.* lately, 7.58. [OE *neowe.*]

NIGHT, *n.* the dark part of a day, night, nighttime, 3.9, 27, 103, 5.27, 7.114, 8.39; **nightes**, 1.51, 7.171. [OE; cp. A *næht*, WS *neaht*, late OE *niht.*]

NOBILL, *adj.* possessing hereditary rank, lofty, exalted in character, 4.22, 7.18; wealthy, 8.65. [L *nobilis.*]

NOGHT, *pron.* & *adv.* nothing, naught; none; not, not at all, 1.16, 21, 24, 25, 47, 56, 3.48, 62, 85, *etc.* [OE *nawiht*, *naht*, *nowiht*, *noht.*]

NOKES, *n.* the corner area of a room or field; a secluded spot, 7.5. [?ON]

NOMEN, *v.* to take, 9.53. [OE *niman.*]

NONE, *pron.* no person; no one, 3.56, 69, 5.68, 9.18, 19, 47, 11.17. [OE *nan.*]

NORTH, *n.* the northern cardinal point or its direction, 7.8, 9.3. [OE *norþ.*]

NOUMBER, *n.* a number, 3.82. [AF *noumbre.*]

NOW, *adv.* at the present time, 1.31, 37, 39, 66, 2.T1, 4, 15, *etc.* [OE *nu.*]

NOWTHER, *adj.* not either, not one or the other, 7.100, 8.75, 8.78. [OE *nahwaether.*]

OBOUT, *prep.* on all sides of, surrounding, 1.30, 84, 2.15, 4.63, 6.36, 7.96, 8.68, 9.61. [OE *abutan.*]

OGAINES, *prep.* in opposition to, against, 1.14; **oganis**, 4.38; **ogaynes**, 3.94, 98. [OE *ongen, agen.*]

OGAYN, *adv.* into a former state or condition, once more, 1.15; **ogayne**, 3.36. [OE *ongan, agen.*]

OKES, *n.* the British oak, 4.62. [OE *ac.*]

OLIVE, *adj.* alive, having life, 5.44, 45. [OE *on life.*]

OMANG, *prep.* amid or among, 7.110, 142. [OE noun phrases *on gemong* & advs. & preps. *gemong, gemang.*]

OPON, *prep.* upon, 1.56, 3.76, 121, 6.4, 7.38. [ON *app* & *a.*]

ORDANIS, *v.* to arrange, make arrangements, 4.5. [OF *ordener, ordon(n)er.*]

OTHER, *pron.* the second of two persons; the second of several persons, things, 1.42, 3.16, 69, 81, 4.53, 10.8; **others**, 7.81. [OE *oþer.*]

OUT, *adv.* with reference to motion or direction outwards, out of, from, 2.1, 3.68, 5.13, 58, 60, 73, 6.47, 7.8, 92, *etc.* [OE *ut* & *ute* adv.]

OUTEN, *prep.* in phrase *withouten*, lacking, with no, none of, 7.47. See OWTEN.

OVER, *adv.* across, over the surface, 7.9, 82. [OE *ofer.*]

OWAY, *adv.* from a place, out, away, at a distance, 5.36, 7.116, 117. [OE *on weg, aweg.*]

OWTEN, *prep.* in phrase *withouten*, lacking, with no, none of, 3.100, 4.35, 11.15. [OE *with* & *utan.*]

PALAYS, *n.* a luxurious dwelling of a ruler or noble; a palace, 7.166. [OF *palais, pales* & L *palatium.*]

PALET, *n.* the head, 7.130. [OF *palet* & ML *palettus.*]

PALL, *n.* stately dress, rich vestments, robe, 7.110. [L *pallium.*]

PAS, *v.* survive with, move ahead, proceed, escape, 3.56, 7.130. [OF *passer.*]

PAVILIOWNES, *n.* a tent, especially a large or elaborate one used for military encampments, 11.32; **pavilyoune**, 4.63. [OF *paveillon.*]

PAY, *n.* satisfaction, liking, pleasure, 3.10. [OF]

PELERS, *n.* plunderers, pillagers, despoilers, thieves, 2.15. [OF *pillëor* & *pilen.*]

PENCELL, *n.* a small pennon, usually attached to a lance; a small company standard, 7.46. [OF *penoncel.*]

PERE, *n.* a pear, wild or cultivated, 1.16, 17. [OE *pere.*]

PERE, *n.* a peer, an equal, 3.14. [OF *per.*]

PESE, *n.* peaceful relations between people, concord, 1.92. [OF *pais, paix, pes.*]

PINE, *n.* pain or injury resulting from punishment; intense longing or grief, trouble or suffering, 7.77, 11.20. [Prob. OE; cp. OE *pinian.*]

PITAILE, *n.* foot soldiers, infantry, 7.56. [AF *pedail* & CF *pietaille.*]

PLACE, *n.* a particular part of space; locality, spot, 8.48, 49, 9.53. [OF *place* & ML *placea.*]

PLAINE, *n.* a field of battle; a field used for a tournament, 1.83. [OF *plain.*]

PLATE, *n.* plate armor worn by a knight or by a foot soldier, 7.46. [OF *plate* & ML *plata.*]

PLAY, *n.* merriment, disport; joy, pleasure, 1.71, 7.108. [OE; cp. WS *plega.*]

PLAY, *v.* to act on, 5.34. [OE *plegan.*]

PLAYNE, *adj.* clear, visible, evident, 3.35. [L *platus.*]

PLEYN, *v.* to complain, make moan, lament, 7.76. [OF *plaindre.*]

POINTES, *n.* object, end, goal; also purpose, intention, 3.46. [OF *point.*]

POLLED, *v.* of persons or their heads: having the hair cropped or shorn, tonsured, 7.131. [From *polle* n.]

POMP, *n.* ostentatious display of wealth, power, strength, 1.16. [OF *pompe* & L *pompa.*]

POPLE, *n.* persons; everyone, all people, 3.19. [OF *pueple*; AF *peple, people.*]

POUER, *adj.* having little or no wealth, 3.122. [OF *povre.*]

PRAIS, *v.* to extol, worship, 7.109, 146; **prays**, 5.59. [OF *preisier.*]

PRAY, *n.* prey, victim, 1.38. [OF *preie.*]

PRAY, *v.* to offer supplication, to pray, 5.16, 35, 9.16. [OF *preier.*]

PRAYER, *n.* a prayer, supplication, 5.35. [OF *priiere.*]

PRELATES, *n.* an ecclesiastic of high rank, 3.17. [OF *prelat* & *prelatus.*]

PRESE, *n.* a crowd, throng, company, an assembly, 1.90, 7.45, 109. [OF *presse* & ML *pressa.*]

PREST, *adj.* ready, prepared; also, ready for battle, armed, 5.61, 7.25, 8.67. [OF *prest.*]

PRIDE, *n.* unreasonable self-esteem, pride; confidence in or reliance on, 4.64, 5.51, 7.44, 45, 108, 109, 9.49, 10.8, 11.32. [Late OE *pryte.*]

PRIKED, *v.* to ride a horse, esp. at a gallop; to spur, 2.15. [OE *prician.*]

PRINCE, *n.* a ruler, sovereign, 7.18; **princes**, 3.16, 19, 44, 4.76, 79, 7.25, 110, 111. [OF]

PRISE, *n.* value, superiority; fame, renown; good reputation, 1.17, 4.26. [OF *pris.*]

PRIVÉ, *adj.* private, secret, 7.5. [OF *privee.*]

PROFERD, *v.* to make an offer or a proposal, 3.23. [OF *porofrir, profrir* & AF *profrer.*]

PROPER, *adj.* suiting, fit, 7.25. [OF

propre.]

PROUD, *adj*. guilty of the sin of Pride; haughty, arrogant, 1.90; **prowd**, 7.110. [OE *prut, prud*.]

PROVE, *v*. to test, to try, 4.15, 5.61; **proved**, attempted, 7.42. [OE *prut*.]

PUPLE, *n*. persons; everyone, all people, 8.67. See POPLE.

PURPOS, *n*. one's object, aim, or goal, 8.39; **purpose**, 11.23. [AF *purpos*.]

PURVAY, *v*. to provide for the supply of some necessity; furnish provisions, 4.34. [AF *purveier*.]

PURVIANCE, *n*. preliminary arrangement, preparation, management, 7.146. [AF *purvëaunce* & CF *porvëance*.]

PUT, *v*. to cause, to set, place in a specific position, 3.95, 7.77, 11.20; **puttes**, 11.32. [OE; cp. *pytan* & *putung*.]

QUELL, *v*. to kill, slay, 1.78, 5.24. [OE *cwellan*.]

QUIT, *v*. to pay, make compensation or amends, 7.66. [OF *quiter, quitter, quettier*.]

QUITE, *adj*. excused, exempt, free; compensated, 7.124, 125. [OF *quite*.]

RADE, *v. pt. 3rd. sg*. to ride, to travel over, through, 7.T2, 47, 9.2. See RIDE.

RAILED, *v*. as *adj*. bestrewn, arranged, set, 4.83. [OF *reillier*.]

RAPELY, *adv*. hastily, quickly, swiftly, fast, 6.67. [ON]

RAPES, *n*. a strong, heavy cord, a rope, 8.68. [OE *rap*.]

RATHLY, *adv*. quickly, swiftly; readily,

7.91. [From *rathe, adj*.]

RAW, *n*. a horizontal, linear arrangement or array, battle order, 4.79, 5.48. See ROW.

RECHE, *v*. succeed in reaching by stretching, 7.15. [OE *ræcan*.]

REDE, *n*. advice, 3.23. [From OE *v. ræden*.]

REDE, *n*. the color red, 8.41. [OE *read*.]

REDE, *v*. to advise, 10.19. [OE *ræden*.]

REDE, *v*. to read aloud, recite from, 7.1. [OE *ræden*.]

REDLES, *adj*. without advice, uncounseled, ill-advised, 6.14, 37. [OE *rædles*.]

REDY, *adj*. prepared, ready, 1.32, 33, 3.89, 4.24, 83, 7.93, 9.23, 43. [From OE *ræde, geræde*.]

REGHT, *n*. that which is morally right; that which is just, royal perogative, 6.78. See RIGHT.

REN, *v*. to run, 6.37, 7.91, 8.6. [OE *rinnan*.]

RENOWNE, *n*. fame, renown; glory, 8.81, [OF *renom, renon*, AF *renoun*.]

RENT, *n*. revenue from property, income, 6.13. [OF *rent* & *rente* & ML *renta*.]

RESE, *n*. haste, 7.47. [OE *ræs*.]

RESON, *n*. the intellectual faculty, intellectual power or capacity, reason, 10.27. [OF]

REST, *n*. rest due to sleep; repose, slumber, 3.33, 5.62, 7.24. [OE *rest, ræste*.]

REST, *v*. to be supported by, to lie on; to cease, remain still, 6.75, 7.163.

[From *n.*]

REVED, *v.* to rob, plunder, despoil; take by violence 3.122, 9.24, 10.18. [OE *reafian.*]

REWFUL, *adj.* pitiable, sad, grievous, 6.38; **rewfull**, 6.13. [From *reu(e n.*]

RICHE, *adj.* rich, wealthy, prosperous; powerful, mighty, great, 4.25, 79, 7.154. [OE *rice* & OF *riche.*]

RIDE, *v.* to ride, to travel over, through, 6.67, 9.10, 17. [OE *ridan.*]

RIFILD, *v.* to rob, plunder, steal; ransack, pillage, despoil, 2.16, 17. [OF *rifler.*]

RIG, *n.* the back of a person, 7.81. [OE *hrycg, hrygc, etc.*]

RIGHT, *n.* a just legal claim, that which is legal and moral, 1.31, 3.7, 28, 4.51, 8.37. [OE *riht.*]

RIGHT, *adj.* in accordance with law, justice, or other standards, 4.28, 6.54. [OE *riht.*]

RIGHT, *adv.* properly, exactly, justly, 7.1, 11, 8.24. [OE *riht.*]

RIGHTWIS, *adj.* just, fair, honest, rightful, 7.113. [OE]

RIVELING, *n.* a rawhide shoe or boot; a derogatory nickname for a Scot, 2.19. [OE *rifeling.*]

ROBBED, *v.* to rob, plunder; carry off, 3.123, 9.24, 10.10, **robbing**, 8.6. [OF *rober, robber.*]

RODE, *n.* the Cross, 6.75, 11.9. [OE *rod.*]

ROMANCE, *n.* a written narrative of the adventures of a knight, a chivalric romance, 7.1, 169, 8.T1. [OF *romanz*; AF *romance.*]

ROUT, *n.* a body of attendants or followers, retinue; a host of soldiers, troops, 1.33, 2.16, 17, 4.89, 6.38; **rowt**, 1.32, 7.94. [OF *rote, route*, AF *rute.*]

ROW, *n.* a horizontal, linear arrangement or array, 4.83. [OE *raw.*]

RUGHFUTE, *adj.* rough-foot, rough-shod, 2.19. [OE *ruh, rug(e.*]

RYE, *n.* cereal grain, rye, 1.20. [OE *ryge.*]

SAD, *adj.* grave, sober, serious, 5.2. [OE *sæd.*]

SAI, *v.* to say, utter, 7.73. See SAINE.

SAID, *v.* to say, utter, 1.43, 46, 3.88, 5.8, *etc.* See SAINE.

SAIL, *n.* length of canvas on sailing vessel to catch wind, 5.25. [OE *segl.*]

SAILED, *v.* to travel on water in a ship, 5.67, 10.13; **sayland**, 5.60. [OE *seglan, seglian.*]

SAINE, *v.* to say, utter, 1.81; **sais**, 5.88, 7.169, 8.T1. [OE *secgan.*]

SAKE, *n.* out of consideration for, on behalf of, 5.2, 6.76, 7.18, 11.9. [OE *sacu.*]

SAKLES, *adj.* innocent, guiltless; blameless, 2.3. [OE *sacleas.*]

SALUE, *v.* to salute, greet, 5.4. [OF *salver.*]

SAND, *n.* sand; a sandy beach; shore, 3.1; **sandes**, 5.71. [OE *sand.*]

SARE, *adj.* sore, painful, 1.15. [OE *sar.*]

SARE, *adv.* sorely, 5.12, 13, 8.60. [OE *sar.*]

SARI, *adj.* painful, 7.88; **sary**, 1.72, 73, 5.28. [OE *sarig.*]

SATT, *v.* to be in a sitting position, be seated, 9.35. See SIT.

SAUL, *n.* soul, spiritual nature of mankind, 3.3; **saules,** 3.114; **sawls,** 5.88. [OE *sawol.*]

SAVE, *v.* to afford or bring about safety; to deliver from danger; rescue, 1.34, 3.2, 22, 125, 4.11, 20, 5.16, 6.81, 8.30, 96, 11.37. [OF *sauver, salver* & L *salvare.*]

SAW, *v.* to see with the eyes, catch sight of, 3.75, 7.79, 89. See SE.

SAWES, *n.* familiar saying, 5.2, 9.56. [OE *sagu.*]

SAWLS, *n.* soul, spiritual nature of mankind, 5.88. See SAUL.

SAY, *v.* to say, to utter, 1.65, 3.36, 5.31, 9.15, 11.25. See SAINE.

SAYLAND, *v.* to travel on water in a ship, 5.60. See SAILED.

SCHAC, *v.* to cause to quiver or tremble, 4.30. [OE *sceacan.*]

SCHAME, *n.* the feeling of having offended against propriety or decency; embarrassment or revulsion, 1.64, 2.12, 3.123, 4.12, 5.16, 8.84. [OE *sceamu, scamu, etc.*]

SCHAWES, *n.* a thicket, a small wood, branches, 11.2. [OE *sc(e)aʒa.*]

SCHELD, *n.* a shield, 1.14; **schelde,** 4.50, 7.105. [OE *scild, sceld.*]

SCHELTRON, *n.* a group of soldiers or an army in fighting formation, squadron, 5.63; **schilterouns,** 6.6. [From OE *scild-truma, etc.*]

SCHENDE, *v.* to disgrace, confound, ruin, 6.21; **schent,** 9.26, 27. [OE *scenden.*]

SCHENE, *adj.* bright, splendid, gleaming, beautiful, glittering, 5.63, 6.6, 7.105, 11.2. [OE *sciene.*]

SCHENT, *v.* to disgrace, confound, 9.26, 27. See SCHENDE.

SCHEW, *v.* to exhibit in public, display; lay open to view, 7.12, 11.2. [OE *sceawian.*]

SCHILTEROUNS, *n.* a group of soldiers or an army in fighting formation, 6.6. See SCHELTRON.

SCHIPHERD, *n.* a shepherd, in phrase *schipherd staves,* a shepherd's staff; also pl. used fig. of people, 9.20. [OE *sceap-hirde.*]

SCHIPMEN, *n.* a sailor, seaman, 3.49, 5.67. [OE *scip-mann, scyp-mann.*]

SCHIPPES, *n.* a sea-going vessel; a vessel used in military expeditions, 1.19, 3.91, 5.71. [OE *scip, scyp.*]

SCHOPE, *v.* of the Deity: to create, bring into existence, 3.1. [OE *scippan, scieppan, etc.*]

SCHOTING, *v.* to shoot, discharge a weapon; archery, 5.49. [OE *sceotan.*]

SCHOWRE, *n.* an abundant flow, 9.43. [OE *scur.*]

SCHREWES, *n.* a rascal, rogue; a wicked person, scoundrel, 9.26, 27. [Prob. OE *screawa.*]

SCHRIVE, *v.* to make confession, confess, 10.20. [OE *scrifan.*]

SCORE, *n.* twenty, a score; twenty persons, 7.57. [OE *scoru.*]

SE, *n.* the expanse of salt water covering much of the earth, sea, 3.1, 7.9, 11, 15; **see,** 10.T2, 4. [OE *sæ.*]

SE, *v.* to see with the eyes, catch sight

of, notice, 3.118, 7.70. [OE *seon, sion*.]

SEGE, *n.* the act or process of besieging a city or castle, a siege, 7.171, 8.T2. [OF *sege*.]

SELDOM, *adv.* infrequently, rarely, seldom, 4.14. [OE *seldan*.]

SELF, *n.* self, 9.50. [OE *self*.]

SEMBLAND, *n.* external appearance; outward show or display, deportment, 7.104, 8.79. [OF *semblant, samblant*.]

SEMBLED, *v.* to come together, congregate, assemble for battle, 3.87. [shortened form of *assemblen*. Cp. OF *sembler*.]

SEMELY, *adj.* pleasing to the eye, fitting, handsome, 6.5; **semly**, 8.28. [ON]

SEMID, *v.* to appear, to give the impression, 4.61, 5.49. [ON *saema*.]

SEN, *adv.* since, from one time until a later time, 1.72, 3.109. [OE *siththan*.]

SEND, *v.* to dispatch, send, 1.7, 7.31; **sendes**, 11.33; **sent**, 1.19, 3.49, 4.47, 5.20, 6.11, 65, 9.16, 21. [OE *sendan*.]

SENE, *v.* to see with the eyes, catch sight of, notice, 2.3, 4.14, 7.104, 8.79. See SE.

SENT, *v.* to dispatch, send, 1.19, 3.49, 4.47, 5.20, 6.11, 65, 9.16, 21. See SEND.

SERE, *adj.* different, various, diverse, 9.56. [From ON]

SERGANTES, *n.* an officer in a lord's retinue; a soldier; a foot soldier, 5.22, 8.28. [OF *serjant, sergant, etc.*]

SERVIS, *n.* obedience required by service to another; willingess or desire to be of service, 9.43. [OF *servise,*

servis(se, etc.]

SET, *v.* to put in a state, 10.20; **sett**, 7.68. [OE *settan*.]

SEVYN, *num.* the cardinal number seven, 4.38. [OE *seofon*.]

SEXTY, *num.* the cardinal number sixty, 3.98. [OE *sixtig, sextig*.]

SHAME, *n.* the feeling of having offended against propriety or decency; embarrassment or revulsion, 1.65. See SCHAME.

SIDE, *n.* a side of something; lateral face; surface of an object, 1.19, 6.65, 8.24; **sides**, 1.15, 7.52; **syde**, 3.74, 6.12, 11.33. [OE]

SIGHED, *v.* to sigh, moan: expressing sorrow, grief; love-longing, 7.157; **sighing**, 6.11. [back formation from *sight(e*.]

SIGHT, *n.* the faculty of sight, ability to see; the range of vision, 1.27, 5.28, 6.5. [OE *sihþ*.]

SILVER, *n.* the metal silver, 10.12. [OE *seolfor*.]

SIN, *n.* sin, offense, violation, transgression, 3.115; **sins**, 6.81; **syn**, 4.12, 6.76, 9.30, 10.20, 11.9. [OE *syn(n)*.]

SING, *v.* to sing, esp. expressing joy or merriment, 5.5; **songen**, 7.138. [OE *singan*.]

SITE, *n.* a feeling of anguish, grief, acute anxiety, 7.65. [From ON]

SITTES, *v.* to be in a sitting position, be seated, 1.1. [OE *sittan*.]

SKARLET, *n.* a kind of rich cloth, cloth of scarlet color, 10.12. [OF *escarlate*.]

SKRITH, *v.* to go, travel, come; to fall, slip, slide, escape, 5.68. [OE *scridan* & ON]

SLA, *v.* to kill, as in battle, 1.46, 3.55; **slaine**, 7.156; **slogh**, 2.3, 3.61, 97. [OE *slean*.]

SLAKE, *v.* to relax, soften, mitigate; to relieve, alleviate, 5.4; **slaked**, diminished, 1.53, 5.5; **slaken**, 9.49. [OE *slacian*.]

SLAYNE, *v.* to kill, as in battle, 7.54. See SLA.

SLIKE, *adj.* like, such, 1.26, 62, 8.35. [ON *slik-r*.]

SLOGH, *v.* to kill, as in battle, 2.3, 3.61, 97. See SLA.

SMALE, *adj.* small, little, limited, 1.6, 3.82, 6.64; **small**, 5.80, 11.20. [OE *smael*.]

SMERTED, *v.* smarted; to pain, to cause to suffer, 5.13. [OE *smeortan*.]

SNAPER, *v.* to trip, stumble; fall into error, 10.16. [G *schnappen*.]

SNARE, *n.* snare, trap, 10.16. [OE *sneare*.]

SNAW, *n.* snow, 5.49. [OE *snaw*.]

SNELL, *adj.* keen, active, bold, ready, quick, 5.22. [OE]

SOCORE, *n.* assistance, help, relief, 1.7; *v.* **socoure**, to help, 3.22. [L *succursus*.]

SOGAT, *adv.* thus, in this way, 4.93. [*so* & ON *gate*.]

SOGHT, *v.* to seek; to attack, 3.107, 5.33, 7.65, 8.50. [OE *secan*.]

SOMER, *n.* summer, 11.2; **somers**, 10.7. [OF *sumer*.]

SON, *n.* male offspring, 9.60; **sons**, 3.15; **sun**, 7.28, 8.70, 92. [OE *sunu*.]

SONE, *adv.* soon, shortly, promptly, 1.7, 3.49, 64, 86, 113, 4.47 *etc.*; **sune**, 5.5, 25. [OE *sona*.]

SONGEN, *v.* to sing, esp. expressing joy or merriment, 7.138. See SING.

SORE, *adj.* sore, painful, 7.54, 156. See SARE.

SOROW, sorrow; mental anguish, suffering, confusion, 1.64, 4.12, 5.4, 5, 6.12, 10.20. [OE *sorh*.]

SOWED, *v.* to smart; to grieve or sorrow, 5.12. [*OE *sugian*; cp. OI *sviða*, to smart.]

SOWRE, *adj.* bitter, sour, 9.44. [OE *sur*.]

SOWTH, *n.* south, 7.8. [OE *suth*.]

SPAC, *v.* to utter words, express oneself, 3.20. See SPEKE.

SPACE, *n.* space, room, area, period of time, 7.31. [OF *espace*.]

SPARE, *v.* to spare, refrain from or forbear, 3.54, 4.16, 7.23, 121, 8.23, 10.1; **spared**, 8.13. [OE *sparian*.]

SPECHE, *n.* that which is spoken, speaking, utterance, 7.121, 8.23. [OE *spec*.]

SPEDE, *v.* to help, aid, prosper, succeed, 1.33, 10.1, 11.38. [OE *spedan*.]

SPEKE, *v.* to utter words, speak, 7.122, 10.1; **spekes**, 2.31. [OE *specan*.]

SPERE, *n.* spear, weapon, 1.14, 3.96, 4.50, 7.105, 8.13. [OE]

SPILL, *v.* to waste, allow to run off, 2.33. [OE *spillan*.]

SPREDE, *v.* to scatter, to disperse, 1.37. [OE *sprædan*.]

STAF, *n.* staff, long weapon, 7.100;

staves, 9.20. [OE *stæf*.]

STALWORTHLY, *adv.* stoutly, sturdily, robustly, 5.43, 8.86; **stalwortly**, 4.50. [OE *stælwierde*.]

STAND, *v.* to stand; to be placed; to exist, to have a specified position, 11.33; **standes**, 5.74; **stonde**, 9.11; **stode**, 3.75, 5.75, 10.30. [OE *standan*.]

STANE, *n.* a stone, rock, 2.32. [OE *stan*.]

STAREAND, *v.* staring, to gaze wide-eyed, 3.67. [OE *starian*.]

STAVES, *n.* staff or cudgel, 9.20. See STAF.

STEDE, *n.* place, stead, position, 1.54, 3.24, 7.50, 8.43. [OE *stede*.]

STEDE, *n.* steed, spirited horse, 4.69, 7.100, 9.35, 11.15; **stedes**, 7.101, 9.11. [OE *steda*.]

STELE, *n.* steel, hard metal, 3.102. [OE *stele*.]

STELE, *v.* steal, take illegally, 3.84, 8.14. [OE *stelan*.]

STEREN, *adj.* stern, firm, unyielding, 2.13. [OE *styrne*.]

STERNES, *n.* stars, 3.67. [ON *stjarna*.]

STIF, *adj.* strong, firm in purpose, unyielding, 4.76, 7.50. [OE *stif*.]

STIK, *v.* to stab, to kill by piercing, 8.14. [OE *stician*.]

STILE, *n.* stile, steps leading over a wall, 1.88. [OE *stigel*.]

STILL, *adv.* quietly, up to the time that, 3.121, 4.5; *adj.* without movement, calm, at rest, 2.32, 3.87, 4.94, 5.75, 6.57, 7.101, 8.54. [OE *stille*.]

STINT, *v.* to stop, end, 5.43. [OE *styntan*.]

STIRT, *v.* to hasten, to set out, 11.15. [OE *styrtan*.]

STODE, *v.* to stand, 3.75, 5.75, 10.30. See STAND.

STOLE, *n.* stole, long scarf worn over both shoulders by priests and bishops, 7.138. [L *stola*.]

STONDE, *v.* to stand, 9.11. See STAND.

STOP, *v.* to cause to halt, to cease, 6.56. [OE *stoppian*.]

STOUND, *n.* time, a short time, a while, 5.75. [OE *stund*.]

STOUT, *adj.* proud, arrogant, boastful; brave, bold, 1.28, 40, 54, 2.13, 5.48, 7.99, 10.30. [OF *estout*.]

STOWRE, *n.* a fight, an armed conflict, 1.89. [AF *estur*.]

STRATE, *adj.* narrow, strict, rigid, 6.56. [OF *estreit*.]

STREME, *n.* stream, brook, river, waterway, 5.74; **stremis**, 3.73. [OE *stream*.]

STREMERS, *n.* long narrow flags, 5.75. [From OE *stream*.]

STRENKITH, *v.* to strengthen, support, aid, 6.77; *n.* strength, 10.30. [See OE *strengthu*.]

STRETES, *n.* streets, public way or thoroughfare, 2.25. [OE *stræt*.]

STREVYN, *v.* to struggle, contend, fight, 8.86. [OF *estriver*.]

STRIF, *n.* strife, contention, dissention, 3.4; **strive**, battle, 5.43. [OF *estrif*.]

STRIKE, *v.* to sound, to be struck, 4.80. [OE *strican*.]

STRIVE, *n.* battle, 5.43. See STRIF.

Glossary

STROKES, *n.* blows, 4.61. [OE *strac.*]
STRONG, *adj.* strong, having great
physical strength, 7.101. [OE *strang.*]
STROY, *v.* to destroy, 3.48. [OF
destruire.]
STUMBILDE, *v.* to stumble, blunder,
make mistakes, 1.88; **stumbill**, 7.99.
[ON **stumla.*]
SUM, *adj.* some, 1.17, 2.32, 3.62, 5.2,
7.150; *pron.* an indefinite number or
specified portion, 1.55, 3.65, 67, 68, 99.
[OE *sum.*]
SUN, *n.* male offspring, 7.28, 8.70, 92.
See SON.
SUNE, *adv.* in the future, shortly, 5.5,
25. See SONE.
SUTH, *n.* truth, 1.76, 81, 3.71, 5.31,
7.37, 8.58, 9.15; *adj.* true, 5.2. [OE
soth.]
SUTHWEST, *n.* southwest, 5.60. See
SOWTH.
SWELT, *v.* to die, 11.9. [OE *sweltan.*]
SWERD, *n.* sword, 8.13, 61. [OE
sweord.]
SWETE, *n.* that which is pleasing,
pleasant, 9.44. [OE *swete.*]
SWIM, *v.* to swim, 5.58. [OE
swimman.]
SWINK, *v.* to work, toil, 4.86. [OE
swincan.]
SWIRE, *n.* the neck, 8.68. [OE
sweora.]
SWITH, *adv.* quickly, 5.67, 8.51, 9.43.
[OE *swiþ.*]
SWORE, *v.* to swear, to make a
solemn declaration, 3.26, 30. [OE
swerian.]
SYDE, *n.* a side of something; lateral
face; surface of an object, 3.74, 6.12,
11.33. See SIDE.
SYN, *n.* sin, offense, violation,
transgression, 4.12, 6.76, 9.30, 10.20,
11.9. See SIN.
SYRE, *n.* lord, ruler, king, 8.69. [OF
sire.]

TABURNS, *n.* a small drum, tabour,
10.8. [OF *tabourin.*]
TAILE, *n.* tail of an animal, 7.15. [OE
taeg(e)l.]
TAK, *v.* to take into possession, 7.24,
140; **take**, 11.28; **takes**, 8.27; **taken**,
9.34, 52; **tane**, 9.66; **toke**, 3.T2, 33, 45,
8.11, 43; **tok**, 5.18; **tuke**, 6.61. [OE
tacan.]
TALE, *n.* tale, story, report, 1.2, 6.60;
tales, 8.35, 38. [OE *talu.*]
TALKED, *v.* to speak to, 9.38. [OE
talian.]
TAME, *adj.* tame, submissive, civilized,
1.60, 8.87. [OE *tam.*]
TANE, *v.* to take, 9.66. See TAK.
TARETTES, *n.* transport vessel, ship
of burden, cargo ship, supply ship,
3.80. [OF *taret, taride.*]
TECHED, *v.* to teach, to give
instruction to, 9.3. [OE *tæcan.*]
TELL, *v.* to narrate, to give an
enumeration, 1.T1, 2, 76, 2.T1, 3.11,
4.4, 55, 5.19, 7.37, 8.35; **tolde**, 4.77,
7.55. [OE *tellan.*]
TEN, *num.* the cardinal number ten,
3.98. [OE *tyn.*]
TENE, *n.* trouble, sorrow, injury, 5.65,
6.2. [OE *teona.*]
TERES, *n.* tears, act of weeping, 7.91.

143

[OE *tear*.]

THANKED, *v*. to thank, to express gratitude, 3.58, 5.80. [OE *thancian*.]

THAR(E), *adv*. there, in that place, 1.59, 61, 70, 81, 2.3, 22, *etc*. [OE *þær*.]

THARAT, *adv*. by reason of that, 3.42. See THAR(E).

THARBY, *adv*. close, near, in specified relation to, 4.41, 11.20. See THAR(E).

THARE IN, *adv*. therein, 6.74, 8.14, 11.10, 11. See THAR(E).

THAREOBOUT, *adv*. about that, 1.30. See THAR(E).

THARFORE, *adv*. therefore, 1.79, 7.127, *etc*. See THAR(E).

THARTO, *adv*. thereto, 3.8, 32. See THAR(E).

THEDER, *adv*. thither, 3.77. [OE *þider, þæder*.]

THIK, *adj*. thick, 7.155. [OE *thicce*.]

THIN, *adj*. thin, 7.19, 7.155. [OE *thynne*.]

THING, *n*. anything, an object, an entity, 1.71, 87, 3.26, 54, 7.146. [OE]

THINK, *v*. to think, to formulate in the mind, to reason, to see fit, 4.6, 8.36, 11.5; **thoght**, 1.41, 4.33, 51, 5.42, 8.53. [OE *thencan*.]

THOWSAND, *num*. the cardinal number one thousand, 7.50, 55. [OE *þusend*.]

THRE, *num*. the cardinal number three, 8.43. [OE *þreo*.]

THRETES, *v*. to threaten, 2.31. [OE *threat*.]

THRETING, *n*. threatening, expression of threats, 2.30. See THRETES.

THRETTY, *num*. the cardinal number thirty, 7.50, 55. [OE *þritig*.]

THRIVE, *v*. to prosper, flourish, 5.42. [ON *thrifask*.]

THURGH, *prep*. from one side to the other, 1.68, 7.T2, 9.10, 17; by means of, 7.43. [OE *þurh*.]

TIDE, *n*. time, season, chance, 6.61, 11.31; **tyde**, 1.17, 8.26, 10.7. [OE *tid*.]

TIDE, *v*. to happen, to befall, 1.72. [OE *tidan*.]

TIGHT, *v*. to purpose, to determine, fix in one's mind, 6.1. [Orig. unknown.]

TILL, *prep*. to; toward, untill, 3.54, 4.95, 6.54, 8.46, 72, 11.40; *conj*. 5.62, 76, 6.68. [OE *til*.]

TIMBER, *v*. to build, 6.2, [OE *getimbran*.]

TIME, *n*. moment, opportunity, 3.109, 4.6, 7.30; **tyme**, 2.32, 7.152, 8.27, 9.34. [OE *tima*.]

TINT, *v*. to lose, destroy, 7.143. See TYNE.

TITHANDES, *n*. tidings, news, 3.58. [ON *tidhendi*.]

TITHE, *n*. tenth part, 5.70. [OE *teoþa*.]

TOK, *v*. to take into possession, 5.18; **toke**, 3.T2, 33, 45, 8.11, 43. See TAKE.

TOLDE, *v*. to narrate, to give an enumeration, 4.77, 7.55. See TELL.

TORCHES, *n*. torches, light of portable flame, 5.29. [L *torca*.]

TOUN, *n*. town, a city, 3.29, 7.89, 94, 8.88; **toune**, 1.57, 2.7, 7.172, 8.83; **tounes**, 3.44. [OE *tun*.]

TOURE, *n*. tower, Tower of London, 9.41, 52, 66. [OF *tor, tur*.]

TRAIS, *v*. deceive, betray, 7.150. [OF *trahir*.]

TRAISTED, *v.* trusted in, expected, 4.58. [ON *treysta.*]

TREGET, *n.* magic, deceit, 7.136. [OF *tresgiet.*]

TRESON, *n.* treason, betrayal of trust or feudal obligation, 1.76, 7.62, 7.149, 8.38, 11.24. [AF *tre(i)son.*]

TREST, *n.* trust, faith, 7.160. [ON *traust.*]

TREW, *adj.* true, honorable, upright, reliable, 1.1. [OE *treowe.*]

TREWLY, *adv.* truly, sincerely, genuinely, 3.11, 4.4, 7.55. See TREW.

TREY, *n.* trouble, affliction, 6.2. [From OE *v. tregian.*]

TRIP, *n.* a stumble, blunder, false step, 7.159. [From OF *v. tripper.*]

TROMPES, *n.* trumpets, 10.8; **trumpes**, 4.80. [OF *trompette.*]

TRONE, *n.* throne, 1.1. [L *thronus.*]

TROW, *v.* to believe, think, suppose, 6.60; **trowed**, 4.95. [OE *treowian.*]

TRUMPED, *v.* to blow trumpets, 5.29; **trumping**, 5.65. [From *v. trumpet(t)en.*]

TRUMPES, *n.* trumpets, 4.80. See TROMPES.

TRUS, *v.* make ready, pack up, 11.31. [From OF *n. trousse.*]

TUKE, *v.* to take into possession, 6.61. See TAK.

TUNG, *n.* tongue, language, 3.20. [OE *tunge.*]

TURN, *v.* to change one's attention, 2.T1; **turned**, to change, alter, 1.15, 5.65. [OE *tyrnan.*]

TWO, *num.* the cardinal number two, 3.15, 80, 5.71, 7.57. [OE *twa.*]

TYDE, *n.* time, season, chance, 1.17,

8.26, 10.7. See TIDE.

TYME, *n.* moment, opportunity, 2.32, 7.152, 8.27, 9.34. See TIME.

TYNE, *v.* to lose, destroy, 10.18; **tint**, 7.143. [OE *teon.*]

UMSET, *v.* to beset, surround, 7.96. [OE *ymbsettan.*]

UMSTRIDE, *v.* to bestride, ride, 4.69. [*um + stride.*]

UNCURTAYSE, *adj.* uncourteous, unknightly, 7.145. [*un* + OF *curteis.*]

UNDER, *adv.* subject to authority; beaten, defeated, 2.18. [OE]

UNDERSTAND, *v.* to understand, perceive, comprehend, 3.59, 7.92, 8.58. [OE *understandan.*]

UNHALE, *adj.* unsound, unhappy, unwholesome, 6.69. [From OE *hal.*]

UNKIND, *adj.* unnatural, cruel, harsh, 5.11, 7.145. [From OE *gecynde.*]

UNSELE, *adv.* unhappily, unseasonably, 9.27. [OE *unsæl.*]

UNTILL, *prep.* up to the time, 3.39, 114; *conj.* to the point or extent that, into, 7.15, 76. [ON *und.*]

UNTO, *prep.* to, 1.2, 3, 7, 2.22, 3.60, etc. [*un + to.*]

UP, *adv.* up, in a higher position, 3.32, 57, 5.85, 8.74, 77, 11.27. [OE *up.*]

USES, *v.* to employ, to use, 2.30. [OF *user.*]

WADE, *v.* to walk in water, to go through water, 5.56, 57. [OE *wadan.*]

WAIT, *v.* to visit (to bring harm to), to watch, lie in wait, to inflict injury, 1.64. [OF *waitier.*]

WAKE, *v.* to watch, to be anxious, 5.3; **waked**, 1.51; **waken**, 9.33; **wakkins**, to be aroused, 6.10; **wakkind**, 9.50. [OE *wacian.*]

WALKES, *v.* to travel, spread, 8.29; **walked**, 10.9. [OE *wealcan.*]

WALL, *n.* choice, select; of persons, noble, 5.77. [ON *val.*]

WALLD, *v.* would, 4.56. See WILL.

WALLES, *n.* walls, defenses, 6.32, 36. [OE *weall.*]

WAN, *v.* to win, 4.26, 8.56, 11.T2. See WIN.

WANE, *n.* a great number, plenty, 3.93. See WONE.

WANIAND, *n.* the waning of the moon, *fig.* an ominous time, 5.30, 9.25, 10.6. [From *wanien*, v.]

WANTED, *v.* to need, lack, fail to get, 7.103. [ON *vanta.*]

WAPIN, *n.* weapon, 5.36, 7.133, 8.15, 10.2; **wappen**, 9.32. [OE *wæpen.*]

WAPNID, *adj.* armed, provided with weapons, 4.39. [From *wapin.*]

WAR, *adj.* used in impersonal phrase, be wary, cautious, 6.8. [From OE *warian.*]

WARDAINE, *n.* official in charge of a town, town warden, 8.83. [From OE *warder.*]

WATER, *n.* sea, ocean, here, English Channel, 7.82. [OE *waeter.*]

WAY, *n.* a course, direction; means of performing, carrying out an action, 1.67, 3.72, 5.33, 9.18, 19. [OE *weg.*]

WEDE, *n.* garment, clothing, armour, 5.38, 8.5, 9.37, 10.2. [OE *wæd(e.*]

WEDER, *n.* weather, 4.48. [OE *weder.*]

WELE, *adv.* satisfactorily, fully, entirely, 1.36, 41, 2.5, 11, 17, *etc.*; **well**, 5.28. [OE *wel.*]

WELE, *n.* prosperity, happiness, success, 3.18, 52, 6.9, 7.117, 8.16. [OE *we(o)la.*]

WELEFUL, *adj.* prosperous, 8.17. [From *wele*, n.]

WELTH, *adv.* riches, abundance, 7.153; **welthes**, 10.11. [From *weal.*]

WEND, *v.* to proceed, to turn, to go, 1.67; **wende**, 9.19; **wendes**, 11.29; **went**, 3.90, 4.23, 6.9, 9.25, 61; to turn back, **wened**, 3.63; **wend**, 1.67; **wonde**, 9.10. [OE *wendan.*]

WENE, *v.* to suspect, to think, believe, 2.4, 5, 5.66, 6.8, 10.11, 11.1; **wend**, 3.62. [OE *wenan.*]

WENT, *v.* to proceed, to go, 3.90, 4.23, 6.9, *etc.* See WEND.

WEPE, *v.* to weep, to mourn, lament, 11.12; **wepeand**, weeping, 8.60. [OE *wepan.*]

WERE, *n.* war, battle, 1.12, 3.95, 6.31, 7.71, 8.15, 9.50, 10.13. [OF *werre.*]

WERKMEN, *n.* warriors, 10.9. [From *were*, n.]

WERLDES, *n.* world, 8.16. [OE *world, weorold.*]

WERLDLY, *adj.* worldly, material, 3.18. [From *werld*, n.]

WERY, *adj.* weary, exhausted, 3.106. [OE *werig.*]

WERY, *v.* to curse, 2.23. [OE *wiergan.*]

WEST, *n.* Westminster Hall, 9.11, 10.15. [OE]

WESTWARD, *adv.* toward the west, 10.13. [From *west*, n.]

WEX, *v.* to grow, to wax, become, 3.106, 4.48. [OE *weaxan.*]

WHAM, *pron.* who, 11.4. See WHO.

WHARE, *adv. & conj.* at or in a certain place, where, *adv.* 2.7, 3.75, 4.14; *conj.* 3.34, 5.18, 84, 7.135; **whore**, 9.19. [OE *hwær.*]

WHAT, *pron.* which thing, what, 3.88, 7.158, 11.5. [OE *hwæt.*]

WHELP, *n.* whelp, offspring of a dog or wolf, pup, 8.78. [OE *hwelp.*]

WHEN, *adv. & conj.* at what time, when, 3.86, 4.40, 44, 55, 62, 95, 5.6, *etc.* [OE *hwanne.*]

WHETE, *n.* wheat, 1.20. [OE *hwæte.*]

WHI, *adv.* why, for what purpose, 6.22. [OE *hwy.*]

WHIDER, *adv.* whither, to what place, whcrc, 2.21. [OE *hwider.*]

WHILE, *n.* period of time, 1.82, 2.5, 11, 17, 23, 29, 35, 7.137, 8.45. [OE *hwil.*]

WHILK, *adj.* which, 3.46. [OE *hwilc*, *hwelc.*]

WHILS, *conj.* as long as, during the time that, at the same time that, 3.112, 9.12. See also AY. [From OE *hwil.*]

WHILUM, *adv.* formerly, once, 8.5. [OE *hwilum.*]

WHO, *pron.* who, 3.118, 5.69, 6.29; **wham**, 11.4. [OE *hwa.*]

WHORE, *adv.* where, 9.19. See WHARE.

WHOTE, *v.* to become aware of, to know, to learn, 11.4. See WIT.

WIDE, *adv.* over a large area, 1.37, 3.73, 6.10, 8.29, 10.9. [OE *wid.*]

WIFE, *n.* woman, 3.55. [OE *wif.*]

WIGHT, *adj.* valorous, brave, stout, 4.87, 8.5, 9.37, 10.2, 13, 15, 11.T2. [From ON *vigt*, (brave in battle).]

WIKKED, *adj.* evil, vicious, 11.6, 8. [OE *wicca.*]

WIL, *v.* used as an aux. or to imply futurity, will, 4.16. See WILL.

WILD, *adj.* reckless, full of emotion, savage, 1.60; **wilde**, stormy, 5.30. [OE *wilde.*]

WILES, *n.* strategem, trick, 8.55. [ON *wihl.*]

WILL, *n.* deliberate intention, wish, desire, choice, 2.34, 35, 3.88, 116, 5.66, 76, 6.59, 7.103, 8.56, 64. [OE *will.*]

WILL, *v.* used as an aux. or to imply futurity, 1.37, 2.9, 4.17, *etc.* [OE *wyllan.*]

WIN, *v.* to win, to capture, 4.9, 51, 6.78, 7.32, 153, 9.22, *etc.* [OE *winnan.*]

WIND, *n.* wind, 2.33. [OE *wind.*]

WINE, *n.* wine, 1.20. [OE *win.*]

WINTER, *n.* winter, 8.26, 11.1. [OE *winter.*]

WIRK, *v.* to plan, contrive; to effect, achieve, 8.20. [OE *weorcan.*]

WIRSCHIP, *n.* honor, fame, glory, 9.32, 33. [OE *weorthscipe.*]

WISE, *n.* manner, ways, 3.47, 8.95. [OE *wise.*]

WISE, *adj.* judicious, wise, 5.38. [OE *wis.*]

WIST, *v.* to inform, to know, to become aware of, 3.52, 4.44, 5.76, 7.158. See WIT.

WIT, *v.* to inform, to know, to become aware of, 5.20; **witten**, 7.4. [OE *witan.*]

WO, *n.* misfortune; sorrow, grief, woe,

defeat, 3.52, 5.11, 6.10, 7.165, 11.12, 29.
[OE *wa*.]

WODE, *adj*. mad, 6.73. [OE *wod*.]

WON, *v*. to abide, to dwell, 2.23;
wonand, 6.74. [OE *wunian*.]

WON, *v*. to win, to capture, 5.72, 8.95.
See WIN.

WONDE, *v*. to hesitate, shrink, turn
back, 9.10. [OE *wandian*.]

WONDER, *adv*. strangely, wondrously,
1.74. [OE *wundor*.]

WONE, *n*. abundance, 4.37. [ON *van*.]

WONEN, *v*. to win, capture, 7.71,
11.30; **wonnen**, 5.36, 8.16. See WIN.

WONING, *n*. dwelling, habitation, 4.2,
11.8. [From *won* v.]

WORD, *n*. fame, report, rumor,
reputation, renown, 8.29, 10.9; **wordes**,
speech or boasts, 1.28, 45, 47, 2.33, 5.3,
38. [OE *word*.]

WORTH, *adj*. equal to, valued at, 1.16.
[OE *weorth*.]

WORTH, *v*. to become, happen, befall,
2.11. [OE *weorthan*.]

WORTHLY, *adj*. honorable,
admirable, 10.2; **worthli**, 5.38. [From
OE *weorthan*.]

WOTE, *v*. to inform, to know, to
become aware of, 11.8. See WIT.

WOUNDED, *v*. to injure, inflict a
wound, 7.54, 156. [OE *wundan*.]

WOUNDES, *n*. injuries, wounds, 1.91.
[OE *wund*.]

WRATH, *adj*. wrathful, angry, 7.14.
[OE *wræththu*.]

WRECHES, *n*. a wretch, a base, mean,
despicable person, 5.36; **wretche**(s),
2.21, 23, 5.57. [OE *wrecca*.]

WREKE, *v*. to avenge, to take
vengeance on, 11.6. [OE *wrecan*.]

WRETEN, *v*. written, 7.3. [OE *writan*.]

WROGHT, *v*. to plan, contrive; to
effect, achieve, 1.45, 3.120, 6.31, 7.62.
See WIRK.

WROKEN, *v*. to avenge, to take
vengeance on, 2.4; **wrokin**, 2.5. See
WREKE.

WROTE, *v*. to root up, 6.32, 33. [OE
wrotan.]

WROTH, *adj*. wrathful, angry, 3.5, 42,
11.12. See WRATH.

WURTH, *adj*. equal to, 1.24. See
WORTH.

WURTH, *v*. to become, happen, befall,
2.17, 29, 35. See WORTH.

WURTHI, *adj*. honorable, admirable,
5.77. See WORTHLY.

YERE, *n*. year, 3.110, 7.129, 9.58. [OE
gear.]

YIT, *adv*. even, besides, up to a
specified time, 1.49, 2.6, 3.99, 5.29, *etc*.
[OE *giet*.]

YOLDEN, *v*. to yield, 8.89. [OE *gield*.]

YONG, *adj*. young, 3.19. [OE *geong*.]

YREN, *n*. iron, 3.102. [OE *iren*.]

YT, *adv*. yet, 3.10. See YIT.

Other Volumes in the Middle English Texts Series

The Floure and the Leafe, The Assemblie of Ladies, and *The Isle of Ladies,* ed. Derek Pearsall (1990)

Three Middle English Charlemagne Romances, ed. Alan Lupack (1990)

Six Ecclesiastical Satires, ed. James M. Dean (1991)

Heroic Women from the Old Testament in Middle English Verse, ed. Russell A. Peck (1991)

The Canterbury Tales: Fifteenth-Century Continuations and Additions, ed. John M. Bowers (1992)

Gavin Douglas, *The Palis of Honoure,* ed. David J. Parkinson (1992)

Wynnere and Wastoure and *The Parlement of the Thre Ages,* ed. Warren Ginsberg (1992)

The Shewings of Julian of Norwich, ed. Georgia Ronan Crampton (1994)

King Arthur's Death: The Stanzaic Morte Arthur and *The Alliterative Morte Arthure,* ed. Larry D. Benson and Edward E. Foster (1994)

Lancelot of the Laik and *Sir Tristrem,* ed. Alan Lupack (1994)

Sir Gawain: Eleven Romances and Tales, ed. Thomas Hahn (1995)

The Middle English Breton Lays, ed. Anne Laskaya and Eve Salisbury (1995)

Sir Perceval of Galles and *Ywain and Gawain,* ed. Mary Flowers Braswell (1995)

Medieval English Political Writings, ed. James M. Dean (1996)

Four Middle English Romances: Sir Isumbras, Octavian, Sir Eglamour of Artois, Sir Tryamour, ed. Harriet Hudson (1996)

To order please contact:

MEDIEVAL INSTITUTE PUBLICATIONS
Western Michigan University
Kalamazoo, MI 49008–3801
Phone (616) 387–8755
FAX (616) 387–8750